Tales *from the* Heart

Also by the author

Heremakhonon
Segu
Children of Segu
Tree of Life
I, Tituba, Black Witch of Salem
Crossing the Mangrove
The Last of the African Kings
Desirada
Windward Heights

Tales
from the
Heart

True Stories
from My Childhood

Maryse Condé

Translated from the French by
Richard Philcox

Published by Soho Press, Inc.
853 Broadway
New York, NY 10003

Library of Congress Cataloging-in-Publication Data

Condé, Maryse.
[Coeur à rire et à pleurer. English]
Tales from the heart : true tales from my childhood / Maryse Condé ;
translated from the French by Richard Philcox.
p. cm.
ISBN 978-1-56947-347-4
1. Condé, Maryse—Childhood and youth.
2. Authors, French Guadaloupe—20th century—Biography.
I. Philcox, Richard II. Title.
PQ3949.2.C65 Z46413   2001
843'.914—dc21
[B]

Printed in the United States of America

10 9 8 7 6 5 4

To my mother

"Remembrance of things past is not what we retrieve from the mind."

Marcel Proust, *Contre Sainte-Beuve*

Tales from the Heart

1

Family Portrait

If someone had asked my parents what they thought about the Second World War, they would have no doubt replied it was the darkest period they had ever known. Not because France was cut in two or because of the camps in Drancy or Auschwitz, or the extermination of six million Jews and all those crimes against humanity that are still being paid for, but because for seven long years they were deprived of what meant the most to them: their trips to France. Since my father was a former civil servant and my mother was still working as a teacher, they were regularly entitled to a paid vacation from their home in Guadeloupe to the *métropole* with their children. For them France was in no way the seat of colonial power. It was truly the Mother Country and Paris, the City of Light that lit up their lives. My mother would cram our heads with descriptions of the marvels of the Carreau du Temple and the Saint-Pierre market, throwing in as a bonus the Sainte-Chapelle and Versailles. My father preferred the Louvre and the Cigale dance hall, where as a bachelor he had gone to get his juices flowing. So we were only halfway through 1946 before they set sail again in sheer delight on the steamship that was to carry them to Le Havre, the first stop on their way back to their country of adoption.

I was the very youngest. One of the family's mythical stories was the circumstances of my birth. My father was still going strong at sixty-three. My mother had just celebrated her forty-third birthday. When she missed her period she thought it was the first sign of menopause and rushed over to her gynecologist, Dr. Mélas, who had delivered her seven times. After examining her, he burst out laughing.

"I was so ashamed," my mother would tell her friends, "that during the first few months I walked around like an unmarried mother and tried to cover myself up."

However much she showered me with kisses, saying that her little "latecomer" had become her walking stick in her old age, I had the same feeling every time I heard this story: I had not been desired.

Today, I can imagine the somewhat unusual sight we must have made, sitting in the sidewalk cafés of the Latin Quarter in a gloomy postwar Paris: my father, a former Don Juan, still looking good for his age, my mother decked out with lavish Creole jewelry, their eight children, my sisters, eyes lowered, rigged out like shrines, my teenage brothers, one of them already in his first year at medical school, and me, a spoiled, precocious little brat. Their trays balanced on their hips, the *garçons de café* would hover around us admiringly like honey bees. Setting down the *diabolos menthe*, they never failed to come out with: "You speak excellent French, you know!"

My parents bore the compliment without turning a hair or smiling, merely a nod of the head. Once the *garçon* had gone, they turned to us as witnesses: "Yet, we're as much French as they are," my father sighed.

"Even more so," my mother continued vehemently, adding by way of explanation, "We're more educated. We have better manners. We read more. Some of them have never left Paris, whereas we have visited Mont Saint-Michel, the Riviera, and the Basque coast."

There was something pathetic in this conversation which, though I was very young, upset me. They were complaining of a serious injustice. For no reason, the roles were reversed. The white-aproned, black-vested *garçons* scrambling for tips considered themselves superior to their generous customers. They were endowed with this French identity which was denied my parents, refused them despite their good appearances. As for me, I could not understand why such people, so proud and pleased with themselves, part of the Establishment back home, were competing with some *garçon de café* who was serving them.

One day I decided to get things straight. Whenever I was in a quandary I would turn to my brother Alexandre, who had renamed himself Sandrino "to sound more American." At the top of his class, his pockets stuffed with love letters from his girlfriends, Sandrino was the sunshine of my life. He was a protective, loving brother. But I would have liked to have been more than just his little sister— forgotten as soon as a bit of skirt flashed past or a soccer match began. Could he explain my parents' behavior? Why were they so envious of people who, in their very own words, couldn't hold a candle to them?

We lived in a ground-floor apartment on a quiet street in the Seventh Arrondissement. It wasn't like in La Pointe, in Guadeloupe, where we were kept locked up at home. In Paris our parents allowed us to go out as much as we liked and even play with other children. At the time I was amazed by their attitude. Later I understood that in France our parents had no reason to fear we would speak Creole or take a liking to the *gwoka* drums like the ragamuffins in La Pointe. I can remember it was the day we were playing tag with the blond-haired children on the second floor and sharing their tea of dried fruit in a Paris still plagued with food shortages. Darkness began to transform the sky into a starry sieve. We were getting ready to go home before one of my sisters put her head out the window and cried: "Children! Papa and Maman say it's time to come in!"

Before giving me an answer, Sandrino leaned back against a carriage entrance. A dark shadow fell over his jovial face, still bearing the chubby cheeks of childhood. His voice turned serious. "Don't worry your head about it," he blurted out. "Papa and Maman are a pair of alienated individuals."

Alienated? What did that mean? I didn't dare ask. It wasn't the first time I'd heard Sandrino poke fun at my parents. My mother had pinned a photo she'd cut out of *Ebony* over her bed. An African-American family with eight children like ours stood for all to admire. All doctors, lawyers, engineers, and architects. In short, the pride of their parents. This photo sent Sandrino into fits of mockery, convinced he would become a famous writer and little knowing that he would die before life had barely laid hands on him. He never showed me the first pages of his novel, but he would recite his poems that left me puzzled, which, according to him, was what poetry should do. I spent the following night tossing and turning in my bed at the risk of waking my sister, Thérèse, who slept in the top bunk bed over my head. I worshiped my father and mother, I reasoned to myself. It was true I was none too pleased with their graying hair and wrinkles. I would have preferred them to be younger. For my mother to be mistaken for my older sister like my best friend Yvelise's mother when she took her to catechism. It was true I was in agony when my father peppered his conversation with Latin phrases which, I discovered later, could be found in the *Petit Larousse Illustré*. Verba volent. Scripta manent. Carpe diem. Pater familias. Deus ex machina. I especially suffered from the stockings two tones too light for her dark skin that my mother wore in the heat. But I knew the fondness at the bottom of their hearts and I knew they were endeavoring to prepare us for what they believed to be a wonderful life.

At the same time I had too much faith in my brother to doubt his judgment. From his expression and tone of voice I sensed that the mysterious word *alienated* designated a type of shameful ailment like gonorrhea, perhaps even fatal, like the typhoid fever last year that carried off so many folk in La Pointe. At midnight, after piecing all the clues together, I came up with a vague theory. An alienated person is someone who is trying to be what he can't be because he does not like what he is. At two in the morning, just as I was dropping off, I swore in a confused sort of way never to become alienated.

As a result, I woke up a completely changed little girl. From a model child, I became a child who answered back and argued. Since I did not quite know what I was aiming for, I merely contested everything my parents suggested: An evening at the opera to listen to the trumpets in *Aïda* or the bells in *Lakmé*; a visit to the Orangerie to admire Monet's *Nymphéas*; or quite simply a dress, a pair of shoes, or ribbons for my hair. My mother, whose virtue was not patience, did not skimp on the number of cuffs she dealt out. Twenty times a day she would exclaim: "Good Lord! What has gotten into the child?"

A picture taken at the end of that particular visit to France shows us in the Luxembourg Gardens. My brothers and sisters all in a row. My father, sporting a mustache, dressed in an overcoat with a fur collar. My mother smiling with all her pearly-white teeth, her almond-shaped eyes squinting under her shiny, rabbit-skin fedora. Standing between her legs, skinny me, disfigured by that sulky, exasperated expression I was to cultivate until the end of my adolescence, until the hand of fate, that always comes down too hard on ungrateful children, made me an orphan at the early age of twenty.

Ever since, I have had plenty of time to understand the word *alienated* and especially to wonder whether Sandrino was right. Were my parents alienated? To be sure, they took no pride in their African ancestry. They knew nothing about it. That's a fact! During their visits to France my father never set foot in the Rue des Ecoles, where the journal *Présence Africaine* was the brainchild of Alioune Diop. Like my mother, he was convinced that only Western culture was worthy of existence and was ever grateful to France for allowing them to obtain it. At the same time, neither one of them felt the slightest inferiority complex because of their color. They believed they were the most brilliant and the most intelligent people alive, positive proof of the progress achieved by the Black Race.

Was that the meaning of "alienated"?

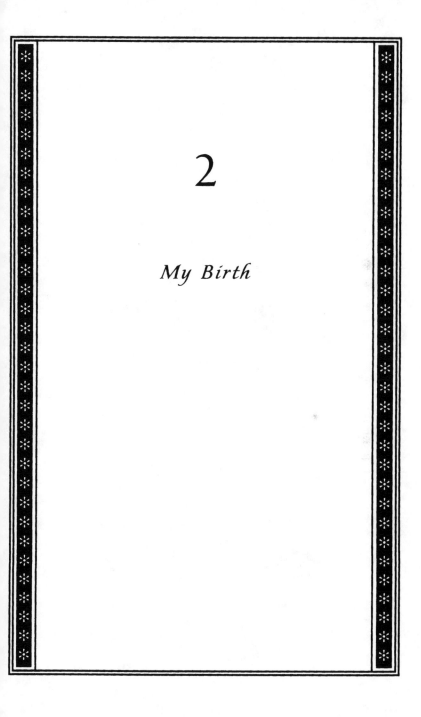

2

My Birth

True to his nature, my father had no preference and couldn't care less whether I turned out to be a boy or a girl. As for my mother, she wanted a daughter. The family already had three daughters and four sons. It would even things up. Once she had gotten over the shame of being caught in flagrante delicto in the pleasures of the flesh at her respectable age, my mother was overjoyed at her condition. Proud even. Her body had not withered and dried up. Her tree of life could still bear fruit. She watched in delight in front of her mirror as her belly rounded and her breasts filled out, as soft as a pair of turtle doves. Everyone complimented her on her beauty. Her blood was infused with a burst of youth that made her eyes and skin glow. Her wrinkles faded away as if by magic. Her hair grew and grew, as thick as a forest, and she brushed it into a chignon humming (a rare thing) an old Creole song she had heard her mother sing, her mother who had died five years earlier:

Sura an blan,
Ka sanmb on pijon blan

Sura an gri,
Ka sanmb on toutewel,

But her condition soon worsened into a difficult pregnancy. No sooner were the bouts of nausea over than the vomiting began. Then the insomnia. Then the cramps. Crab claws cut into her calves. After the fourth month she was exhausted, soaked in sweat from the slightest movement. Feebly holding her parasol she lugged her body through the torrid heat of the dry season as far as Dubouchage, where she stubbornly kept up her teaching routine. At that time there was no such thing as maternity leave: four weeks before delivery, six weeks after or vice versa. Women worked right up to the day before giving birth. When she arrived worn out at the school, she collapsed with all her weight into an armchair in the principal's office. Deep down, the principal, Marie Célanie, was of the opinion that having sex after forty was no longer acceptable, especially with a bag of bones for a husband. All right for the young. However, she kept these uncharitable thoughts to herself. She dabbed the sweat from her colleague's forehead and gave her a medicinal mint spirit diluted in ice water. The burning mixture got her breath back and my mother set off for class. Her pupils were quietly waiting for her in a state of apprehension, instead of kicking up their usual rumpus. With heads lowered over their writing exercises they painstakingly applied themselves as if it were the most normal thing to do.

Fortunately, in addition to Sundays and its high mass that had become a chore, she could rest on Thursdays. On that day my older brothers and sisters were instructed to make themselves scarce. My mother kept to her bed, a mountain of flesh under embroidered linen sheets in the darkness of her bedroom behind closed shutters. The fan hummed. By about ten, Gitane had finished trailing her feather duster over the furniture, beating the rugs and drinking her nth cup of weak coffee. She then carried up pitchers of hot water and helped my mother with her toilette, seating her in a zinc bathtub, her belly with its barbaric-looking navel bulging out in front of her. Gitane scrubbed her back with a clump of leaves, then wiped her down with a bath towel, powdered her in a white flour of talc like a fish about to be fried, and helped her slip on her hemstitched cotton nightdress. After that my mother went back to bed and dozed until my father came home. However hard the cook worked on producing succulent little dishes of chicken breast, conch vol-au-vent, squid pastries, or crayfish in sauce, my mother would send the trays away in desperation, craving fish fritters.

Not disheartened, the cook hurried back to her kitchen range while my father returned to reading the *Nouvelliste,* impatient with his wife for coddling herself too much, but careful not to reveal his thoughts. Around two in the afternoon, after a hurried kiss on her damp forehead, he left the bedroom, which smelled of orange blossom and asafetida, with a feeling of liberation, and found himself out in the blazing sun. How lucky he was to have been spared all those disgusting things like menstrual periods, pregnancies, childbirth, and menopause! Satisfied at being a man he swaggered across the Place de la Victoire. People recognized him for what he was—a conceited individual. Without committing any real crime, my father went back to visiting the friends he had stopped seeing because my mother disapproved of them. He resumed his passion for playing *belote* and dominoes, which she thought beneath him, and smoked a lot of Montecristo cigars.

In her seventh month, my mother's legs began to swell. One morning she woke up with two tree trunks for legs crisscrossed with swollen veins, hardly able to move. It was a serious sign of too much albumin. Straightway, Dr. Mélas prescribed complete rest, no teaching, and a very strict diet without a grain of salt. From that moment on my mother fed herself on fruit. Sapodillas. Bananas. Grapes. And above all, apples from France, round and red like the cheeks of the baby on the Cadum soap posters. My father ordered them by the crateload from a friend who had a business on the wharf. The cook stewed them, baked them with cinnamon and brown sugar, and battered them. The sickening smell of these overripe fruit permeated the entire house from the ground floor to the bedrooms on the third and made my brothers and sisters feel nauseated.

Every afternoon around five my mother's best friends came and sat around her bed. Like my father, they, too, thought my mother coddled herself too much. So they turned a deaf ear when my mother began whining, and carried on about all the christenings, the weddings and funerals in La Pointe. "Can you imagine, my dear, Pravel's hardware store went up in flames like a match. They retrieved the charred bodies of five workers out of the ashes and Monsieur Pravel, a heartless white Creole—aren't they all?—couldn't care less. They're talking about a strike." My mother, who in normal times took little interest in social issues, took even less interest now. She suddenly sat up: I had moved inside her. I had given her my first kick. Good Lord! If, God forbid, I was a boy, I'd be a first-rate soccer player.

My mother's time finally arrived. She was so huge she could no longer fit into the bath and spent her time in bed or in her rocking chair. She had filled three wicker baskets with my things and passed them round to her friends to admire. In one the batiste, silk, and lace blouses, the crocheted booties, the baby's cape, bonnets, and bibs all in pink. In the other, the vests and diapers either in toweling or simple cotton triangles. In the third, the embroidered sheets, the coverlets and the towels. There were also jewels in a pretty papier mâché box: a chain bracelet (unengraved, naturally), a chain necklace with its bunch of holy medallions, and a cute little brooch. Then the visitors would tiptoe into the holy of holies, my room, a former closet adjoining my parents' bedroom, refurbished especially for me. My mother was very proud of a print on one of the walls of the Visitation with the angel Gabriel holding a lily, which I contemplated throughout my childhood, and of a night lamp standing on my bedside table in the shape of a Chinese pagoda that glowed pink.

It was now Carnival time and La Pointe was heating up. In fact there were two carnivals. The respectable one with young maidens in costume and processions of floats around the Place de la Victoire, and the other one, the rowdy one, the real one. On Sundays, gangs of masked dancers, the *mas*, emerged from the outlying neighborhoods and converged on the center of town. *Mas à fèye, mas à konn, mas à goudron.* Moko zombis perched on their stilts. Whips cracked. Whistles pierced eardrums and the beat of the *gwoka* drums rattled and spilled the sun's bowl of yellow oil. The *mas* capered down the streets, inventing a thousand pranks. The crowds on the sidewalks fought to get a view. The fortunate few crowded onto their balconies and threw them coins. During this period it was impossible to keep Sandrino inside the house. He disappeared. Sometimes the maids who went looking for him found him drunk, his clothes smudged with stains that not even Eau de Javel could get out. But those occasions were rare. Usually he reappeared at nightfall and, without a groan, submitted to the thrashing administered by my father.

Around ten on the morning of Mardi Gras my mother was gripped by what she thought to be the pain of her first contractions. They soon, however, abated and eventually the pain lessened. Dr. Mélas, who had been hurriedly called for, assured her after an examination that she would not go into labor before the following day. At lunchtime she ate the cook's fritters with a healthy appetite, even asked for more, and drank a glass of sparkling wine with my father. She had enough energy to lecture Sandrino, whom Gitane had just caught by his shirttails at the corner of the Rue Dugommier. Shortly, the Good Lord would bestow on him the gift of a little sister (or a little brother) for whom he would be responsible for guidance and good example. This wasn't the moment to act like a hooligan. Sandrino listened with that look of skepticism he reserved for all my parents' speeches. He had no inclination to serve as an example to anyone and couldn't care less about a new baby. But, he assured me, he loved me at first sight when a few hours later he saw how ugly and puny I was, dressed in my outfit worthy of a princess.

At one in the afternoon, rushing in from every outlying corner, the *mas* invaded La Pointe. When the first beats of the *gwoka* shook the pillars of heaven, as if she were waiting for that very signal, my mother lost her waters. My father, my brothers and sisters, and the servants went into a panic. No cause for alarm. Two hours later, I was born. Dr. Mélas arrived to receive me, all sticky, in his large hands. He never stopped repeating to whoever would listen that I popped out without a hitch.

I like to think that my first scream of terror went unnoticed in the midst of the town's rejoicing. I like to think it was a sign, a sign that I would know how to cover up deep grief under a laughing countenance. I harbored a grudge against my older sister Emilia who, too, was born amidst the crackling and glow of fireworks one July 14.

She stole from me what in my eyes made my birth unique. I was christened with great ceremony one month later. According to the custom in large families my brother René and my sister Emilia were my godfather and godmother.

When I was a little girl cuddled up against her on her lap, my mother recounted ten times a day, sparing no detail, the very commonplace incidents that preceded my birth: no eclipse of the sun or moon, no overlapping of stars in the heavens, no earthquakes, no hurricanes. Nothing could make me understand why I hadn't stayed inside her womb. The colors and lights of the world around me were no consolation for the nine months in the dark where I had swum blind and happy with my catfish fins. I had only one desire: to return where I had come from, and consequently rediscover a happiness that I knew I had lost forever.

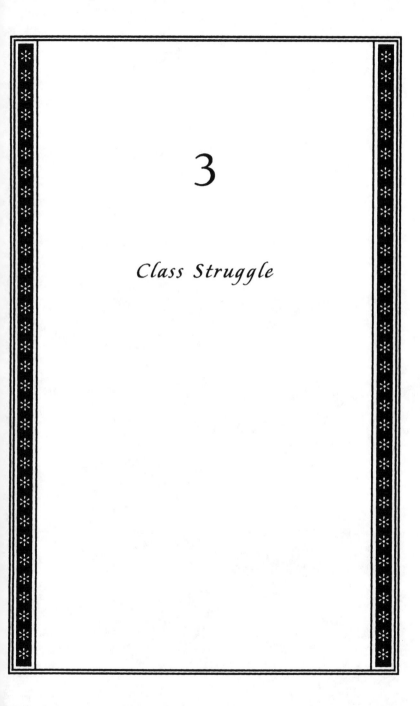

3

Class Struggle

In those days there were no kindergartens or preschools in La Pointe. So small private schools mushroomed. Some gave themselves pretentious names such as "Cours privé Mondésir." Others went by amusing names such as "Les Bambinos." But the one that got the highest rating, where the so-called upper class sent their children, was the school run by the Rama sisters, Valérie and Adélaïde. It was situated in a quiet little street behind the cathedral of Saint-Pierre and Saint-Paul on the ground floor of an upstairs-downstairs house that looked out onto a yard where mango trees provided shade for the pupils' games whatever the season. The Rama sisters were two old maids who at first sight looked identical. Very black, almost blue. Thin, even bony. The hair of each carefully straightened and pulled back into a chignon. Dressed in dark colors, rainy season come dry season, as if they were wives and mothers in mourning. On closer inspection, however, Valérie had a beauty spot over her upper lip bigger than a cufflink, while Adélaïde had a lucky gap in her front teeth when she laughed, and was more relaxed. She sometimes added a lace collar to her dresses and her white petticoat often showed.

Valérie and Adélaïde were well educated. Those who had access to the office they shared on the second floor would gasp in admiration at the leatherbound books that covered the walls from floor to ceiling. The complete works of Victor Hugo. The complete works of Balzac. The complete works of Emile Zola. They could also admire the magnificent pair of side whiskers that enlivened the severe portrait of their late father in a heavy frame. He had been the first black magistrate in Guadeloupe. My mother, who for some unknown reason disliked the Rama sisters, lamented that this fine family was about to die out. Why had neither Valérie nor Adélaïde found a suitor to her liking? My mother had such a reputation that at first the Rama sisters refused to have me as one of their pupils whom they taught to sing *Frère Jacques* and *Savez-vous planter des choux*. They finally accepted on the condition they could administer punishment whenever I deserved it.

"Punishment? I don't want anyone laying a hand on my child," grumbled my mother.

But for once my father had the final say and I was in. The first few years at school were bliss. I had not yet begun to hate it and think of it as a prison where you are bound to conform to meaningless rules and regulations.

In our circles all the mothers worked, much to their great pride. They were generally elementary school teachers and felt sharp contempt for the manual work that had been their mothers' undoing. For us there were no mommies waiting at home in faded slips welcoming us with lavish kisses at the door after a day of washing and ironing the laundry with their red-hot irons or boiling root vegetables and in the evening telling us the Creole tales of Zamba or Rabbit. By age five, we were all too familiar with the misfortunes of Donkeyskin, the fairy tale by Charles Perrault. At seven, the adventures of Sophie. Our fathers, too, left very early in the morning, dressed in ties and starched white drill suits, wearing tropical helmets that didn't stop them from sweating profusely. So the children in our neighborhood had to troop to school under the guidance of a servant. She had to be someone trustworthy. The group of parents rejected outright Olga, the Claviers' servant, who was slightly cracked and belonged to a company of *mas* that raced through the streets, covered in tar, at carnival time. They also rejected the Roseaus' maid, who had the annoying habit of standing on street corners to chat with her admirers. And the Ecanvilles' servant as well, she was too young.

The final choice was Madonne, our very own servant, who was about fifty, a tall, melancholic, high yellow woman who left her six children to fend for themselves on the Morne Udol in order to brew the coffee in our kitchen at five every morning. Madonne was not strict. She was content to walk in front of us, merely clapping her hands from time to time to get my attention, for I was always behind the group, head up, gazing blindly at the glare of the sun, never tiring of imaginary exploits. She allowed me to pick up sandbox seeds on the Place de la Victoire and thread them for a necklace. Instead of taking the direct route, she would take the most roundabout way to school. For all these reasons, we were deeply saddened by the drama that was about to unfold.

One morning, Madonne committed the unpardonable sin of not turning up for work. One of my sisters had to get breakfast ready. Another, take us to school. At the end of the day when we had given her up for good one of her boys knocked on our door. He mumbled in his poor French that his maman had had to take her daughter, who had fallen seriously ill, to the Saint-Jules hospice, and that not only did she need an advance on her wages, but was asking for several days off. My mother made a quick calculation, paid everything she owed, and dismissed Madonne there and then, an attitude that was criticized to varying degrees by the other parents. On the whole they thought my mother was wrong. She was heartless, everyone knew that. After that, I think it was my sister Thérèse who was in charge of taking us to school. One afternoon a few days later, while I was lagging behind the group as usual, I found myself face to face with a tall, hefty boy, or at least that's how he appeared to me.

"Bou-co-lon (he hammered out the three syllables of my name fiercely), *an ké tchouyé-w!*" (I'm going to kill you), he murmured so that only I could hear.

Then he marched toward me with an even more terrifying look, as if he were about to put his words into action. I ran as fast as I could to safety at the head of the little procession. The next morning I didn't see him. At four in the afternoon, though, my heart trembling with fright, I recognized him standing at a street corner. The strange thing was that he looked like any normal child. No dirtier or more untidy than any other. Short-sleeved shirt, khaki shorts, and sandals. I returned home clinging to Thérèse, much to her surprise. The next few days I didn't see him again and hoped it had just been a bad dream. Then he reappeared while I was hopping along minding my own business and murmuring a story to myself. This time he did not merely threaten me. He gave me a punch in the ribs that sent me flying. When my violent screams brought Thérèse running back to me, he had vanished. She was adamant I was lying because I lied all the time, as they said at home. This little game went on for weeks, or so it seemed to me. The boy seldom appeared in the morning and not every afternoon. Just when I thought I would never see him again he loomed up out of the blue, terrifying me even more. Most of the time he was unable to lay a hand on me. So he merely kept his distance, making horrible faces and the most obscene gestures. I began to cry as soon as it was time to venture out of doors and clung desperately to Thérèse's skirts all the way to school. My mother was on the point of taking me to see Dr. Mélas, worried as she was about my constant fits of panic, when Adélaïde Rama eventually noticed a kid hanging around the school after class. When she tried to approach him, he ran off as if he had a guilty conscience. Her description corresponded to mine. He didn't look like a good-for-nothing or a ragamuffin. More like an orphan. They believed me. Henceforth it was my father who escorted me to school. His hand gripped my wrist as tight as a gendarme's handcuffs. He walked so fast that I had to run to keep up with him. He crossed the streets with his giant stride oblivious to the sound of the cars' horns. But the objective was achieved: The boy took fright. He disappeared. Forever.

Everyone had an explanation for the mysterious boy. Who was my aggressor? What did he really want? My parents' version was this: The world was divided into two classes: There was the category of well-dressed, well-heeled children who went to school to learn and become somebody. Then there was the other category of children who were scoundrels and envious, intent on causing harm. The first category therefore must never lag behind and must be constantly on their guard.

I liked Sandrino's explanation better. It was more convincing because it was the stuff of novels. According to Sandrino, he had seen Madonne in our neighborhood several times dressed in deep mourning for her daughter who had died at the Saint-Jules hospice. Her son, outraged at his mother's misfortune and the injustice inflicted upon her by our family, had made up his mind to avenge her. He had vented his anger on me, perhaps in a cowardly fashion, the most vulnerable member of the family.

"The fathers," Sandrino gravely concluded, "have eaten sour grapes and the teeth of the children are on edge."

4

Yvelise

My best friend since elementary school was called Yvelise. Affectionate, as playful as a dragonfly, as good-humored as I was temperamental, so they said. I envied her name that combined her father's and mother's: Yves and Lise. Because I wasn't at all happy with mine. However often my parents drummed it into me that mine was the name of two valiant women pilots who had accomplished God knows what aerial raid shortly before I was born, I was not impressed. When Yvelise and I walked round the Place de la Victoire arm in arm, strangers who were not familiar with family connections in La Pointe asked if we were twins. We did not look alike, but we were of the same color: not too black, not red either, same height, both gangly, all spindly legs and bony knees, often dressed the same.

Although some ten years younger, Lise was one of my mother's best friends. They held the same desirable status in society: Both were elementary-schoolteachers married to men of means. But whereas my mother could rely on a spouse without reproach, Yves was a dedicated womanizer. Lise had never been able to keep a servant girl or a good friend, except for my mother. Yves had given a bun in the oven to every one of the little country girls whose families had entrusted Lise with their education. In fact when Lise and my mother got together my mother would always have to listen to a poignant tale of marital misfortune, and then administer advice. She did not beat about the bush and urged divorce with a generous alimony. Lise turned a deaf ear because she adored her handsome man, however much he fooled around.

I was in seventh heaven when Yvelise left Les Abymes and came to live on the Rue Alexandre-Isaac. In a house close to ours and almost as nice. Two stories painted blue and white. Potted bougainvillea on the balcony. Electricity. Running water. On the excuse I was helping her with her homework, I constantly hung out at her place. I would have liked to live there. Her mother, too taken up with her marital troubles, left us alone. The few times her father was home he joked around with us good-heartedly. He certainly wasn't a pedant like my father. And it wasn't difficult to get her three brothers to drop their shorts and show me their weenies. They even let me touch them sometimes.

In the mornings, under the alleged supervision of her brothers, who were too busy chasing after girls to look after us, we trotted off together to our new school, the Petit Lycée. I can remember these rambles across town when it seemed we were in a realm of our own. The sun frothed like white rum. The sailing ships bound for Marie-Galante huddled in the harbor. The market women seated solidly and squarely on the ground tempted us with topi tamboos and dannikites. Cane juice was sold in tin goblets. The Petit Lycée had just opened on the Rue Gambetta and our parents, out of pure vanity, wanted to be the first in line to enroll us. I wasn't happy there. First of all, I had lost prestige as the daughter-of-one-of-the teachers. Secondly, it was cramped. It had once been a family home like the one we lived in. Bathrooms and kitchens had been turned into class-rooms. It was impossible for us to run around yelling in the tiny recreation yard where we quietly played hopscotch.

At school everything conspired to separate me from Yvelise.

It's true we were in the same class. It's true we sat side by side in our often identical dresses. But whereas I sailed through first in everything, Yvelise was always last. If her parents hadn't been who they were she would never have been admitted to the Petit Lycée. Yvelise didn't read, she droned. She thought for a long time before discovering the solution to the mystery of two plus two. Her dicta-tions had fifty mistakes. She was incapable of memorizing a fable by La Fontaine. When the teacher called her up to the blackboard, she wriggled and fumbled so helplessly that the class roared with laugh-ter. She was only good at music and singing, for the Good Lord had endowed her with the voice of a nightingale. The piano teacher chose her to sing the barcarole solo from *The Tales of Hoffmann*. The fact that Yvelise was a hopeless pupil had no effect on our relationship. It merely awakened my protective instinct. I was her fearless knight in armor. Anyone who made fun of her had to deal with me first.

I was not the only one at the Petit Lycée to take Yvelise under her wing. Our schoolteacher, Madame Ernouville, loved her for her sweet nature. Whereas she hated me because of my unruly ways, especially the way I poked fun at everyone à la Sandrino, even people, she pointed out, who knew more than I did, Yvelise was her little darling. She had more than once urged the principal to caution Lise that I wasn't the sort of company to keep. She wasn't my idea of good company either. She was squat and fat. Light-skinned like an albino. She spoke with a nasal and guttural accent, transforming all her *r*'s into *w*'s, placing a *y* in front of every vowel and opening wide her *o*'s. When giving a dictation she pronounced the word *period* as *pe-wiod*. She was the complete opposite of my mother, as well as of my idea of a woman.

I was convinced Yvelise and I were friends for life, a friendship built on a solid rock foundation. Yet out of spite and a twisted mind Madame Ernouville almost brought it to an end.

In December, lacking even more imagination than usual, she asked us to write an essay on the very unoriginal subject "Describe your best friend."

The topic bored me. I rushed through it and didn't think any more about it once I had handed it in. A few days later Madame Ernouville began giving back the corrected homework with the verdict: "Maryse, eight hours of detention because of all the nasty things you wrote about Yvelise."

Nasty things? Thereupon she began reading my essay out loud in her grating voice: "Yvelise is not pretty. She's not intelligent either." The other girls giggled and cast sideways glances at Yvelise who, hurt by this blunt candidness, was squirming in her seat. Madame Ernouville went on reading. With the same clumsiness, my essay tried to explain the mysterious friendship between a dunce and an exceptionally gifted pupil. In fact, matters would have not gone further than a few snickers and a quick sulk by Yvelise, who was too good-hearted to take umbrage, if Madame Ernouville had not decided to write a report for the principal on what she called my nastiness. Outraged, the principal informed Yvelise's mother, who took my mother to task violently for the way she brought me up. I had called her daughter an ugly halfwit. Who did I think I was, eh? I was the worthy offspring of a family who was stuck-up, a family of niggers who thought themselves superior to everyone else. My mother took offense. My father too. Yvelise's father in turn got into a huff. In short, the grown-ups entered the dance and forgot the origin of the squabble between us children. The outcome was that my mother forbade me to set foot inside Yvelise's home.

I had to obey and was in agony. Friendship between children has the passion of love. Deprived of Yvelise, I was racked by constant pain like a throbbing toothache. I couldn't sleep. I couldn't eat and my dresses hung shapelessly. Nothing amused me: neither my brand-new Christmas presents nor Sandrino acting the clown, not even the matinee shows at the Renaissance. Even I, who loved the cinema, was unmoved by the Shirley Temple films. In my head I wrote Yvelise a thousand letters of explanation and apology. But why apologize? What was I being blamed for? For having told the truth? It's true Yvelise wasn't exactly a beauty. Her mother soulfully reminded her of it at the slightest occasion. It's true she was no good at school. Everyone knew that.

The Christmas vacation lasted an eternity. Finally the Petit Lycée opened its doors again. Yvelise and I were back in the recreation yard together. By the mournful look she shyly cast in my direction and her unsmiling mouth, I knew she had suffered as much as I had. I went over to her and offered her my chocolate bar.

"Do you want half?" I begged in a whisper.

She nodded and held out her hand in forgiveness. In class we took up our usual places and Madame Ernouville did not dare separate us.

To this day, except for the eclipse of adolescence, my friendship with Yvelise has survived other dramas.

5

The Bluest Eye

The Rue Alexandre-Isaac where our house was located began a little farther up from the Place de la Victoire, the very center of La Pointe's social life, and vanished into a respectable working-class neighborhood. Not at all like the Vatable Canal district, with its open ditches and shacks. It was a venerable street, inhabited by old established families but also by those of modest means yet with impeccable manners. My parents had moved there a few months before I was born, when the house on the Rue Condé had become too small for the growing number of children, but above all because it no longer corresponded to their new standing. My father had just been decorated with the Légion d'honneur, goodness knows why, and my mother had proudly sewn red thread on every one of his buttonholes. "Monsieur Boucolon,"—as someone had once asked him—"what's that red on your jacket?" she liked to repeat, holding her sides with laughter.

The houses on the Rue Alexandre-Isaac were built of wood with identical frames. Yet there were subtle differences, such as the shade of red of the zinc roofs, a fresh coat of paint, or the splash of flowers along the balconies, that distinguished one from the other. A family of twelve children, the Driscolls, occupied a vast corner house, badly maintained with a patched roof and an empty balcony without bougainvillea or hibiscus. Whenever they met my parents there would be a polite "Good morning" or "Good evening." But they never mixed. Deep down, my parents felt superior to them. M. and Mme. Driscoll were obscure civil servants, without class, who didn't even own a car. It was rumored they were odd and not like other people. And then they were mulattos. At that time in Guadeloupe you didn't mix. Blacks went with blacks. Mulattos with mulattos. White Creoles went their own way, and the Good Lord was content up in Heaven. Luckily, the children did not bother too much with grown-ups' business. We lived on good terms with the Driscolls of our own age, however mulatto they might have been, and Gilbert could have been my first boyfriend.

He was a somewhat frail little boy with curly hair like an Arab street urchin's, and his shyness contrasted with the behavior of his rough-and-tumble brothers.

I had never heard the sound of his voice and I imagined it wafting over the hills like a flute. We first met at catechism during an Easter retreat with sixty other children. Ever since, we conveyed our feelings by casting adoring looks at each other for hours on end from our respective balconies. On Thursday mornings we kept a low profile because our families crowded onto the balconies. Madame Driscoll rested her weary bones in a chaise longue or else cradled the latest newcomer to the family. My sisters dug their embroidery needles into the linen table sets. The Driscoll boys did their homework. But in the afternoon, it became too hot to stay out among the potted plants. Everybody retreated inside for their siesta and lowered the *persiennes.* The little market at the corner finished its business for the day. The local shops closed up, and the only person left wandering in the street was a mad man nicknamed Banjo because of his bulging hernia. My mother, in a cotton shift, already resting under her mosquito net, impatiently called out: "Come in, for goodness sake! What are you doing out in the sun like a sheet being bleached?"

I didn't budge. Gilbert, however, put on sunglasses, covered his head with an old *bacoua* hat, or shaded himself under a parasol. As for me, I didn't dare move, for fear of arousing suspicion, and I stoically continued to sweat profusely under the hammering sun. After months of risking sunburn, Gilbert grew bolder. Unlike me, who had told nobody, he confided in his best friend Julius, one of Yvelise's brothers. I had recently fiddled with Julius's weenie, amazed at the way it stiffened between my fingers, but there was never any pretense of a deeper attachment. It was just a game and a physical initiation. One late afternoon Julius managed to outwit prying eyes and slip me an envelope. It contained an amazing photo. At first sight, it appeared to be a picture of a dog: a huge Alsatian, sitting on its hind legs, jaws wide open and tongue hanging out. Then in the left-hand corner I made out Gilbert, bare-chested, so tiny he looked like an elephant boy beside his charge. The photo must have been taken two or three years earlier and he can't have been more than six years old. His bangs down to his eyes, he was smiling with a toothless grin. On the back of the photo he had written the magic words: "I love you." I hid my treasure in a small wicker basket under my stuff for church, the only place my mother did not regularly inspect. Then I racked my brains thinking what I could give him in exchange. My family had a preference for group photos: the eight children between Papa and Maman, or else my brothers with my father or my sisters and me around my mother. There was no picture of me alone. Not even with a dog. So what could I give him? A handkerchief I had embroidered? A shell I'd painted? A raffia belt I'd woven? I was hopeless with all ten fingers. I collected zeros for manual work. I ended up choosing a tortoiseshell barrette my mother used to adorn my hair with.

Now that his love had been officially declared and approved, Gilbert sent me a letter by the same messenger. At first sight, nothing extraordinary. It was written on pretty blue stationery in a firm hand. No ink blobs. As homework, the strictest of teachers would have marked "Very neatly written." I began to read with beating heart. But it stopped at the very first line: "My darling Maryse, you are the loveliest of them all with your blue eyes."

I thought I had misread. Blue eyes? Me? I ran to the bathroom and looked at myself in the mirror. Undeniably, my eyes were dark brown. Not even light brown. Almost black. I returned to my room and sat down on the bed. I was troubled. It was as if I had read a letter meant for someone else. Throughout dinner I was so unusually glum and silent that someone remarked: "Good Lord, is the child coming down with a fever?"

I went back up to my room and reread the letter. The wording hadn't changed: "My darling Maryse, you are the loveliest of them all with your blue eyes."

This time I did not want to confide in Sandrino who, I knew, would burst out laughing and treat me to one of those convoluted explanations he was so good at. What had happened? Had Gilbert taken a good look at me? Had he wanted to make fun of me? Was he trying to be clever? I was so angry that when Julius came back for an answer I handed him a note with a pompous phrase found in

one of my sister's favorite romance novels: "Gilbert, it's all over between us."

I had no idea I was committing the same fatal mistake as Gilbert—I
was copying. I was copying out of a cheap novel. To venture into
the unknown terrain of love letters, Gilbert had probably sought
some kind of reference. Alas, our references were French pulp novels.
For fear of catching sight of him on the following days I did not go
out onto the balcony and remained holed up inside. He did not give
up immediately. I ran across him one afternoon on the sidewalk
outside Yvelise's. He had his best friend in tow to give him courage.
I had never been so close to him. He had combed his hair and
splashed himself with Jean-Marie Farina cologne. I realized he had
big, sad, gray eyes.

"What did I do to you?" he murmured in a languishing voice.

But the sound of his voice was not what I had expected. It didn't
match his slender body. It was a gruff voice. Almost a grown-up's. I
was to remember it years later. I remained speechless. I rushed into
Yvelise's and burst into tears on her shoulder, telling her the whole
dismal episode.

6

Mabo Julie

Before losing my *mabo* Julie, I had never come face to face with death. My mother was an only child. My father too. His own father, a sailor in the merchant navy, had abandoned his wife as soon as he had sown a child in her belly. Those children who grow up among a vast tribe of half-brothers, half-sisters, uncles, aunts, cousins, and close and distant relatives are one day confronted with death's terrible grimace. This was not my case.

Is that why death began to exert a fascination over me that has never flagged since? Every time a funeral procession went down the Rue Alexandre-Isaac I ran out onto the balcony to watch it slowly head toward the cathedral. I was not too fond of funerals for the poor accompanied by a handful of loyal relatives to their last resting place, without flowers or wreaths. I liked the funerals that displayed the opulence of those who were now entirely dispossessed, headed by a cloud of choirboys in their winged surplices surrounding the priest, brandishing the cross at arm's length. Followed by the coffin draped in its silver cloth. Among the crowd dressed in black, I only had eyes for the first row, the close relatives, the widows, invisible under yards of crepe, the men, with heavy armbands sewn onto their sleeves, and the children marching mechanically like little robots. Thinking back, it was as if I sensed that I would never attend the funeral of those I held so dear. As if I were trying to imagine what my own mourning would have been like. Sometimes, in those days, musicians accompanied the procession. Some blew on saxophones. Others banged cymbals. And their music was a premonition of my love for requiems today. When *mabo* Julie fell ill with pleurisy and complications of the lungs, my mother was afraid of contagion. So I never visited her and only saw her again on her deathbed.

Mabo Julie was the maid who had cradled me in her arms and walked me round the Place de la Victoire to be admired by all those who had eyes to admire my silk, tulle, and lace blouses. She had helped me learn to walk, picked me up and comforted me whenever I fell. When I no longer needed her, my mother kept her on—she had no means of support—and she did the laundry. She would arrive every Wednesday balancing a tray on her head piled high with spotlessly clean, sweet-smelling clothes. My father, who was so particular about his starched shirt collars, couldn't find a word of reproach. *Mabo* Julie was an old mulatto woman, very white of skin, with watery-colored eyes and cheeks wrinkled like a passion fruit that has lain on the ground three days. I think she came from Terre-de-Haut on the islands of Les Saintes. I never saw her with husband or child, and perhaps this was why she depended on us. As for me, I loved her like my own mother who, I knew, was jealous. Quite wrongly. My feelings for both were radically different. My mother expected too much from me. I was perpetually required to be the best in everything and everywhere. Consequently, I lived in fear of disappointing her. My terror was hearing that unequivocal judgment she too often sentenced me with: "You'll never do anything worth-while with your life!"

She was always criticizing me. Finding me too tall for my age, way above all the other children in my class, too thin, nothing but skin and bones, my feet were too big, my buttocks too flat and my legs crooked. In *mabo* Julie's eyes, however, I didn't need to move a finger to be the loveliest and the most gifted of little girls on earth. My words as well as my deeds were marked with the seal of perfection. Every time I saw her I hugged her so violently her madras headtie came undone, revealing her silky white hair. I showered her with kisses. I jumped up and down on her lap. She opened up her heart and her body to me. In the years before she died, always laid up sick with dysentery, bronchitis, or a fever, she no longer did our laundry and I missed her like an ointment on a wound.

I shall never forget the evening my mother told me in a rather matter-of-fact tone of voice that *mabo* Julie had had a relapse and had passed on. At first I didn't seem to be feeling any grief. I had the strange sensation that the moon was passing between the earth and the sun and that I was in its darkening shadow. I was groping around like a blind person. I could hear my mother asking for my father's opinion. At my age, should I be allowed to attend a wake? See a dead body? They went on debating for ages. They both thought I should be toughened up. I had too much of an attitude. Always whining about next to nothing. Meanwhile my grief was growing and grow-ing, ready to gush out with a force more powerful than a geyser. Finally, my mother decided to take me with her. We were on the point of leaving when Sandrino whispered in my ear with his usual cheekiness: "Watch out! If you don't behave yourself, she'll come and tickle your feet!"

Mabo Julie lived not far away in the Carénage neighborhood, where I had never been before. An old fishermen's district, clustered around the Darboussier factory, which was still operating at that time. Despite the late hour, the street lined with low houses was swarming with people. Children were running in all directions. Market women were selling all kinds of candies, coconut treats, and sweet potato cakes. Sitting on their stoops, men in undershirts slapped down their dice or dominoes yelling: "*An tchou a-w!* Right where it hurts!"

Others were drinking elbow to elbow in the rum shops. To me, all this hustle and bustle was not simply frightening but shocking. You'd have thought that *mabo* Julie's death did not mean a thing to these people. Coming closer to the house of the deceased, whose doors were draped in black, you could hear the hum of voices. *Mabo* Julie's house was tiny. A single room divided in two by a curtain. In the half that served as a bedroom it was as light as day because of all the candles. It was also very hot. The neighbors, who were obscuring the view of the deathbed strewn with flowers, drew aside when they saw my mother. Then I saw *mabo* Julie dressed in her finest clothes, her hair twisted into puffs on either side of her black madras headtie. I didn't recognize her. She was taller. Heavyset. Another person had taken her place. She had lost her smile. She suddenly looked hostile and threatening.

"Kiss her!" my mother ordered.

Kiss her?

I was about to step back. Then I remembered Sandrino's warning. I made an effort to obey. I placed my mouth on the cheek I had kissed so often and to my surprise found it, not warm and soft as usual, but hard and cold. Cold. A cold unlike anything I could describe. Not even ice. Rather a stone. A gravestone. I was filled with mixed feelings: sorrow, fright, and shame of being afraid of someone whom I had loved and who had suddenly become a stranger. I gulped and began to cry. This was not to my mother's liking. She would have preferred I show no emotion in public like a royal child. Irritated, she shook me. "For goodness sake, get a hold of yourself!"

I sniffled. We stayed an hour or two around the corpse. Holding her rosary, my mother prayed. Under the scent of flowers I could smell decomposition. Finally we went home.

That very night my nightmares began. My mother only had to close my bedroom door for *mabo* Julie to enter. Not the Julie I had adored during her lifetime, but the other one, the stranger. Sometimes she lay down beside me in bed. They put me in Thérèse's room, and she was exasperated by all this song and dance. "You're always playing the grown-up when in fact you're nothing but a coward."

I wonder how it would have all ended if one evening my mother hadn't taken me on her lap as she was so good at doing and hugged me while I cried my heart out.

"How can you possibly imagine that a person who loved you so much wants to do you harm? She's like your guardian angel now."

She had probably just remembered that I was only nine years old.

7

History Lesson

Often, after Adélia had served dinner at 7 p.m. on the dot, my father and mother went out arm in arm to enjoy the cool of the evening. They used to stroll down our street as far as the magnificent house of the Lévêques, a family of white Creoles—father, mother, five children, and a maiden aunt gone to seed under her mantilla— whom we saw at mass but the rest of the time seemed to live behind drawn curtains and closed doors. Then they would turn left, passing in front of the Renaissance movie theater, and cast disapproving glances at the posters for the first American films in Technicolor. They hated America, without ever having set foot there, because it was English-speaking and because it wasn't France. They walked round the harbor breathing in the sea air, sauntered as far as the Quai Ferdinand-de-Lesseps, where the smell of codfish always clung to the drooping branches of the almond trees, then returned to the Place de la Victoire, where they sat down on a bench after strolling up and down the Widows' Path three times. They stayed there until nine thirty, then stood up in unison and walked home by the same circuitous route.

They always dragged me with them. Because my mother was quite proud to have such a young child in her late middle age and also because she worried whenever I was out of her sight. I never enjoyed these walks. I would have preferred staying home with my brothers and sisters. As soon as my parents had turned their backs, they began to kick up a rumpus. My brothers would come out and talk to girls on the doorstep. They played beguines on the phonograph and recounted all sorts of jokes in Creole. During our walks my parents never bought me grilled peanuts or coconut candies on the pretext that a well-behaved person doesn't eat in the street. I was reduced to looking longingly at all these delights and stood in front of the women selling them in the hope that they would take pity on me in spite of my clothes from Paris. Sometimes the trick worked, and one of them, her face half-lit by her oil lamp, would hold out a handful: "Here, this is for you, darling!"

During these walks my parents more or less ignored me and talked between themselves. About Sandrino, whom the *lycée* was threatening to expel once again. About one of my sisters who was not working at school. About monies that my father had cleverly invested. And over and over again about the wickedness of people's hearts in La Pointe and how as blacks they were criticized for having succeeded in life. Because of my parents' paranoia, my childhood was lived in a constant state of anxiety. I would have given anything to be the daughter of ordinary, anonymous folk. I got the impression that the members of my family were exposed to a volcano whose burning lava threatened to engulf them at any moment. I hid these feelings as best I could behind a mask of make-believe and turbulence, but they nevertheless kept gnawing at me.

My parents always sat on the same bench next to the bandstand.

If it was occupied by some undesirable individual, my mother would stand rigid in front of him, beating time with her foot with such an impatient expression that he very soon cleared off. I amused myself as best I could. I hopscotched down the paths. I kicked around stones. I spread my arms and became a plane soaring into the air. I called out to the stars and the crescent of the moon. I told myself stories out loud with elaborate gestures.

One evening, in the midst of my solitary games, a small girl emerged out of the dark. Fair-haired, badly dressed, with a mousy-colored pigtail trailing down her back.

"*Ki non a-w?* Whatcha name?" she called out in Creole.

Deep down I wondered who she took me for. Some ragamuffin? Expecting to make some sort of impression, I loudly announced my identity. She did not seem impressed, for it was obvious this was the first time she had heard my name, and continued with the same tone of authority in Creole: "I'm Anne-Marie de Surville. We're going to play together. But my mother mustn't see me with you or else she'll beat me."

I followed her gaze and saw the backs of a group of white women sitting motionless, their hair floating down to their shoulders. I didn't like the manners of this Anne-Marie at all. At one point I was tempted to turn on my heels and go and join my parents. Yet I was only too happy to have found a playmate my own age, even if she did order me around like a servant.

Immediately Anne-Marie took charge of our games, and throughout the entire evening I submitted to her whims. I was the naughty pupil and she pulled my hair. Then she pulled up my dress and gave me a spanking. I was the horse. She climbed on my back and dug her feet into my ribs. I was the servant and she slapped me across the face. She showered me with insults. I shuddered hearing the forbidden cuss words of *kouni à manman a-w* and *tonné dso* fly out of her mouth. In the end I was hurt so badly by a final cuff that I ran to take refuge in my mother's arms. I was too ashamed to explain. I pretended I had had a bad fall and left my torturer capering about unpunished near the bandstand.

The following evening Anne-Marie was waiting for me in the same place. For over a week she never failed to turn up and I meekly surrendered to her torture. After she had almost blinded me in one eye I finally protested, tired of her brutality.

"Stop hitting me!"

She sneered and gave me a spiteful punch in the stomach.

"I have to hit you because you're black."

I had enough strength to sneak away.

On the way home, however much I thought about her answer I couldn't find any sense to it. I got into bed, and after praying to the numerous guardian angels and all the saints in paradise, I asked my mother: "Why is it black people have to be beaten?"

My mother looked amazed and exclaimed: "How can a little girl as intelligent as you ask such a question?"

She hurriedly traced the sign of the cross on my forehead, switched off the light, and closed my bedroom door behind her. The next morning, while my hair was being done, I returned to the subject. I sensed that the answer would provide the key to the often mysterious edifice of my world. The truth would come out of the jar where they had hidden it. Weary from my insistence my mother tapped me with the back of the comb.

"For goodness sake, stop it with your nonsense. Have you ever seen anyone beat your father or me?"

An unlikely idea, but my mother's nervousness betrayed her embarrassment. She was hiding something from me. At lunchtime I stole into the kitchen to pester Adélia. Alas, she was busy making a sauce. As soon as she saw me, even before I could open my mouth, she began shouting: "Out you go, or I'll call your mother."

I had no other choice. I hesitated for a moment then went up and knocked on my father's study door. Whereas I always felt protected by my mother's warm, fussy affection, I knew I was of little interest to my father. I was not a boy. After all, I was his tenth child, for he had two sons by a previous marriage. My tears, whims, and noise exasperated him. I asked my question as if it were a leitmotif. "Papa, why is it black people have to be beaten?"

He looked at me and answered absentmindedly:

"What are you talking about? They used to beat us a long time ago. Go and talk to your mother, will you?"

From that moment on I kept my questions to myself. I was afraid of what Sandrino would say. I guessed that a secret was hidden at the bottom of my past, a painful, shameful secret that would have been wrong, even dangerous, to prise open. It was better to keep it buried deep in my memory like my mother and father, and everyone else I knew, seemed to have done.

The next day and the following I returned to the Place de la Victoire with my parents, determined not to play with Anne-Marie. But however much I looked for her up and down the paths, left and right, she was nowhere to be seen. I ran to the bench where her mother and aunts used to sit. It was empty. I never saw them again. Neither her, nor the group of women.

To this day I wonder whether this meeting was not supernatural. Since so much deep-rooted hatred and suppressed fear remains buried in our islands, I wonder whether Anne-Marie and myself had not been reincarnated as a mistress and her long-suffering slave during the space of our games.

Otherwise how else could I, usually so rebellious, have been so docile?

8

Paradise Lost

When I was nine or ten my mother enrolled me in the "Jean-nettes," a branch of the girl scouts. She thought quite rightly that I wasn't getting enough exercise. Needed toughening up. Always last in gym. In fact, all I did was drag my body four times a day from our house to the Lycée Michelet, and in the evening go and sit on a bench in the Place de la Victoire next to Yvelise, eating cornet upon cornet of grilled peanuts. Apart from that, I spent the rest of my time in my room, *persiennes* lowered, curled up on my sheets, sometimes reading, mostly daydreaming. Putting together unlikely stories with which I filled the heads of anyone who had the patience to listen. I devised incredible miniseries with a regular cast of characters always involved in extraordinary adventures. I maintained, for example, that I was in daily contact with a man and a woman named Lucifer and Lucy. Dressed in black from head to toe, they held a magic lantern to their eyes, and by the light of their candles, told me every detail of their seven lives: from being oxen tied to their stakes in the sa-vanna, to turtle doves flying through the forest, and goodness knows what else. My mythomania caused my mother a great deal of worry.

With hands joined over my prayer book, she made me ask forgiveness from my guardian angel and swear never to deviate from the straight and narrow, which I remorsefully promised from the bottom of my heart. I did not keep my promise because my imagination was my only source of bliss. At my young age, my life was oppressive. It was too orderly. No whims or fantasy. As I said, we had no relatives or alliances. We never had people over. The visits of my mother's friends did little to break the monotony of life. They always looked the same, covered in makeup, decked out in hats and jewels: Madame Boricot, Madame Revert, and Madame Asdrubal. They seldom found grace in my mother's eyes. One of them laughed too loud. Another told racy jokes in front of the children. Another was too fond of dubious puns. Never a family reunion, banquet, feast, or wake. Never a ball, a dance or music of any kind. Deep down, I already had that, "what's the point of it all" feeling, which has seldom left me, and ever since I have tried to escape under a frenzy of activity.

I was only content when I invented a universe of my own.

My mother did not achieve her objective. I began to hate the Jeannettes. First of all, the ill-fitting uniform: deep blue, with a tie and a Basque beret. Then the weekly outings. Every Thursday after lunch Adélia filled a small basket with a gourd of anise-flavored lemonade, a bread twist, a chocolate bar, and slices of marble cake. Together with about twenty other girls under the supervision of a quartet of den mothers, I set out for the Morne de l'Hôpital. We sweated it out in twos for a good half hour under the boiling sun. When we got there we weren't even allowed to cool off under the shade of the tamarind trees. We had to run, jump, follow clues, and sing at the top of our voices. Although I took a dislike to the other Jeannettes, who reciprocated, I adored the den mothers. Especially one of them:

den mother Nisida Léro, from a well-to-do family and unfortunately an old maid at the time, who had a heart of gold in her virgin breast. I don't know what became of her and wish her every happiness in the world with all those children she so much wanted. I was her little pet. She would sit me on her knees and coddle me. In my memory I have the picture of a very dark mulatto woman with the hint of a mustache and an aquiline nose. I loved combing her thick chignon, which was always on the point of cascading down to her shoulders. I can't help thinking she was just as allergic as I was to gymnastics, high jumps, long jumps, and all those sweaty exercises that she had us do with such enthusiasm. She simply believed she had discovered a good way of filling in time until a husband came along.

Sometimes during the long vacation we went camping. Oh, not very far! Never farther than Petit Bourg and its surroundings. Bergette, Juston, Carrère, and Montebello. At the camp, it was impossible to daydream; once up and dressed it was forbidden to set foot inside the tents again. We had to be in perpetual motion. We were constantly doing chores: sweeping, washing up piles of tin plates and beakers, peeling mountains of root vegetables, and searching for wood while the sensitive plants scratched our calves in the savanna. In the evening sitting round the fires, we would trot out insipid tales, while the smoke stung our eyes and throats. Once the flames were extinguished the mosquitoes ate us alive. Every evening I nursed myself to sleep in tears. In those days there was no telephone in Guadeloupe. I couldn't call my mother to tell her how miserable I was and beg her to come and get me. When these endless trips were over (how long did they actually last?), I went home gaunt and emaciated, and for a long time refused to leave my mother's lap.

"Get down, you're suffocating me," she would protest, when I showered her with kisses.

My worst memory remains a stay in Barbotteau in the hills above La Lézarde. There wasn't a single day, I seem to recall, when the jet-black sky did not burst with rain. Unable to erect our tents on the soaked grass, we had to make do with a damp, uncomfortable, and dilapidated building. Perhaps a school. Locked up inside we played at tic-tac-toe and drank herb tea while singing absurd songs: *"Il ne fera plus kokodi kokoda."*

After this stay in hell the moment finally arrived to return home, full of ominous signs that I failed to decipher. The rented bus got stuck in the mud on leaving the camp. Everyone had to get out and push beneath the pouring rain. When we got to Arnouville it ran over a rooster that was crossing the shiny road surface beating its wings, and smashed it into a red pulp. By an extraordinary coincidence, the bridge over the Rivière Salée was up and we had to wait for ages and ages by the side of the road. When we finally arrived at La Pointe it was almost nightfall. The meeting point was always the same: in front of den mother Nisida's house. It was situated in a more residential neighborhood than ours on the other side of the Place de la Victoire, which was a bit like our Fifth Avenue. It was here that servant or mother, depending on the family's rank, retrieved their Jeannette. Some of the girls strutted home to the fold, bragging and inventing all sorts of stories. I, usually so talkative, always returned home with my head down and in silence.

That evening I waited on the sidewalk for over an hour: Nobody came to fetch me. So den mother Nisida took me by the hand and together with her brothers we walked over to the Rue Alexandre-Isaac.

Passing in front of the cathedral of Saint-Pierre and Saint-Paul, standing huge in the darkness, a cloud of bats flew out of their niches of saints and enveloped us—another omen of ill-fortune. Dotted with the market women's oil lamps, the Place de la Victoire had become the realm of those whose dealings are hidden in the shadows. I walked on, my heart beating to the rhythm of mourning. My intuition told me that my suffering had only just begun. We arrived at the corner of the Rue Condé.

My parents' house was plunged in darkness. From top to bottom it was hermetically sealed. The heavy outer doors were drawn shut and double locked. A neighbor, Madame Linsseuil, always spying on other people, informed us from her balcony that my parents had gone to our country house in Sarcelles. When were they expected back? She didn't know. On hearing this I uttered such a terrible cry that other neighbors came out on their balconies, recognized me, and commented that I was big enough to know better than to make such a scene. What with the education I was getting. The future looked promising for my parents if that's how they brought me up! Den mother Nisida paid no attention to their wicked gossip and managed to calm me down with hugs and kisses. I walked back to her house like a zombie, realizing that once again I was going to spend the night without my mother.

Two servants fluttered around the Léro family table, as they sat down to dinner. A very bourgeois family but cheerful nonetheless. The father, an old wizened mulatto, was quite a tease. The mother, just like her daughter, but stouter. The sons, unruly. Granny wearing a mantilla over her snow-white hair. Aunt Cécé with manners like a nun. Two country cousins. One female cousin. They made room for me beside den mother Nisida and everyone outdid themselves to be considerate. If my parents did not return home the following morning, Monsieur Léro promised me his driver would take me to Sarcelles. That night I would sleep in her room, den mother Nisida proposed with a smile. What pretty rings I had in my ears, Madame Léro purred. I didn't hear a word. Out of respect for so much kindness I tried to gulp back my groans and tears. But I had a lump in my throat and couldn't swallow a thing. Absolutely nothing. My plate remained empty. I couldn't touch a single dish. Not the grilled sea bream. Nor the chayote au gratin. Nor the purslane salad. For dessert a servant placed in front of me a ramekin filled with chocolate cream.

I loved chocolate cream.

Forgetting my pain, my eyes dried instantly. I hesitated, infinitely ashamed at surrendering to gourmandise at such a moment. Finally, I made up my mind. Reluctantly, I was about to pick up my spoon when, in a flash, the other servant whisked the cream away and took it back into the depths of the kitchen. I sat flabbergasted.

Why, after over fifty years, does the picture of that gilt-edged blue ramekin filled with a creamy delight I never got to taste go through my mind again and again, a symbol of everything I have desired and never obtained?

9

Happy Birthday, Mummy

My mother's birthday fell on April 28, a date that nothing could erase from my memory. Every year it was an event that, regular as clockwork, was organized like a coronation. At the Dubouchage School, where she had taught for twenty years, her favorite pupils (for she had a loyal following) recited compliments and presented her with a bouquet of roses, her favorite flower, on behalf of the entire class. Back home at lunchtime my father gave her a present, usually a necklace or a bracelet that was added to her already heavy box of jewels. At four in the afternoon the ice cream maker began to churn in the yard. Adélia, who remained stoically good-humored despite her miserable wages, served tea to my mother and her perfumed, spruced up friends. There were bunches of roses everywhere. Then my brothers and sisters, in costume and makeup, performed in front of this audience a short play they had written themselves and rehearsed in utmost secrecy. Finally my father uncorked the champagne, which had been chilling since the day before. For years I had been content to be a kind of busybody, getting in everyone's way. I wanted to lick the cake mold and turn the handle of the ice cream churn. I refused to embrace my mother's friends, but managed to shower her with sticky kisses. I spilled barley water on my dress. I finished off the half-empty glasses. In short, in the words of my sister Thérèse, the only family member who showed no lenience toward me, "I always had to be the center of attention." Gradually as I grew up, I was no longer content with my second-rate role. On reaching the age of ten, I wanted to attract my mother's attention and do something out of the ordinary to deserve her congratulations.

Here perhaps I should try and sketch a portrait of my mother. It's something I have only quite recently been able to do since my mother never said a word about herself. She had neither brothers nor sisters, just a few cousins from Marie-Galante who brought us mandarin oranges on New Year's Day, and since her own mother had breathed her last before I had even breathed my first, it was easy to imagine her emerging from limbo all grown-up to give birth to a litter of siblings.

Her name was Jeanne Quidal. I keep in my memory the picture of a handsome woman. Skin like a sapodilla and a sparkling smile. Tall and statuesque. Always elegantly dressed, except for her stockings, which were a shade too light. In La Pointe few people liked her despite her tireless charity work: She supported dozens of unfortunate wretches who came looking for help every Sunday. She acquired a legendary reputation. Her ever caustic remarks and comments quickly made the rounds. Her fits of temper and bursts of anger were blown out of proportion. The story was spread around that she had broken her parasol over the back of a policeman for his having failed to show respect for her. But underlying her character was her pride. She was the daughter of an illiterate, illegitimate woman—Granny Elodie—who had left La Treille on the island of Marie-Galante to hire her services out in La Pointe. A photo on the Klein piano showed a fragile, head-scarfed mulatto woman, weakened by a life of exclusion and servitude. "Yes, massa. Yes, ma'am." My mother had therefore grown up below the stairs of bourgeois houses, humiliated by the masters' children. She was destined for a life of pots and pans like her mother and a bun in the oven from the first man to come along. But as early as elementary school, the colonial authorities, who are not always blind to the facts, noted her exceptional intelligence. With the help of scholarships and loans she became one of the first black teachers—and a good catch. Much sought after, she could expect a church wedding with veil and bouquet. But she was not easily fooled, fully aware that a great many of her suitors were interested only in her grade-one elementary-schoolteacher's pay.

At the age of twenty she met my father. He was forty-three and prematurely white-haired. He had just buried his first wife and found himself alone with two small boys, Albert and Serge. Nevertheless, my mother agreed to marry him. Although I have nothing to go on, I suspect that love had little to do with her decision. Jeanne did not cherish this widower encumbered with children, who was already racked with arthritis and partially blind behind his thick, tortoise-shell glasses. But the ambitious forty-year-old, who promised to sweeten her life, had built an upstairs-downstairs house on the Rue Condé and owned a Citroën C4. He had resigned from teaching to go into business. With a group of enterprising partners he founded the Caisse Coopérative des Prêts, the future Banque Antillaise, for the benefit of civil servants. On the surface, my parents' marriage was the usual mixture of happiness and unhappiness. They had eight children. Four boys. Four girls. They lost two at a very early age, which my mother never got over. They had money and traveled widely. As far as Italy. My father was a faithful husband. No half-brother or half-sister came round asking for money for school shoes. Yet, I always felt that my father did not deserve my mother. However much he called her "my treasure" he did not understand her, and, what's more, she frightened him. Sandrino, my elder brother, was adamant about it. According to him, my mother was a frustrated and unsatisfied woman.

"What do you expect?" he went on. "She sold herself to an old bag of bones. I bet she hasn't made love properly for years. You, you were an accident."

Beneath her flamboyant appearance, I imagine my mother must have been scared of life, that unbridled mare that had treated her mother and grandmother so roughly. A stranger had raped Elodie, and fifteen years earlier a factory worker on Marie-Galante had sexually assaulted her own mother. Both of them had been abandoned with their "mountain of truth" and their two eyes to cry with. Elodie had never owned anything. Not even a shack. Not even a nice dress. Not even a grave. She slept for eternity in the family vault of her last employers. Consequently my mother was haunted by the fear of sinking to their level. And especially of being taken for common folk and not being respected for what she had achieved through sheer hard work. She terrified my sisters. Only Sandrino and I stood up to her. Even when I was a child, some of her axioms drove me wild. There was one in particular she would repeat to me, especially as I was inclined to keep company with Adélia in the kitchen.

"You'll never do anything worthwhile. Intelligent girls don't spend their time in the kitchen."

I did not understand that it was her way of lamenting the gap that had widened between her servant mother and herself throughout the years. Folk in La Pointe said she was a heartless individual who had broken Elodie's heart. That she treated Elodie like a leper and wouldn't let her come near her children. That she was ashamed of Elodie's head tie and made her wear a hat that bared her thinning temples. Ashamed of her mother's Creole speech, she forced her into silence. Ashamed of her subservient attitude, she hid her every time they had visitors.

At age ten, encouraged by my good grades in French, I asked whether I could read one of my compositions for my mother's birthday. Everyone agreed, as they always did. I did not ask for anyone's help. Not even Sandrino's, who scorned these birthdays and refused to act in the short plays. I had no idea what I wanted to write. I merely sensed that a personality such as my mother's deserved a scribe. That I had to endeavor to portray such a complex character as best I could. After thinking about it for some time, I decided on a poem in free verse, which would be theatrical at the same time. There would be only one character. Through her constant change of moods, the character would express the various facets of my mother's personality. Both generous, ready to give her last penny to some unfortunate individual, and tight-fisted while quibbling with Adélia over a raise of a few francs. Emotional to the point of weeping hot tears over the misfortune of some stranger. Yet arrogant. Quick-tempered. Especially quick-tempered. Capable of killing with her razor-sharp words and incapable of asking forgiveness. For weeks I worked relentlessly, neglecting my schoolwork. I woke up at night and saw the moon as round as a wheel of Brie sitting on the edge of my window. I got up at four in the morning, careful not to arouse the attention of my mother who was already up and dressed in the next room. For without necklace or earrings, as stark as a crucifix, my mother never missed the dawn mass. She took communion once a day and back in her pew, elated, she remained deep in prayer until the *Ite missa est*. What could she have asked of the Good Lord?

After weeks of anticipation the sun finally rose on her birthday. From early morning fate gave me a thousand clues that things would not go as planned. Unfortunately, I was a blind and obstinate child. At the Dubouchage School, the favorite pupils could not remember their text of congratulations and with open mouths, squirmed on one foot then the other—"Like turkeys," my mother flung at them. At lunch my father presented a brooch that clearly was not to my mother's liking and then pricked her when he pinned it to her crepe georgette blouse. Adélia tripped in the kitchen and chipped all the champagne glasses. The short play was a disaster despite the desperate prompting. My mother's limp applause expressed her disapproval. Only my piece remained to make up for the family's lost honor.

This text has since disappeared and I cannot say what it contained exactly. I remember it was strewn with references to classical mythology as I was studying the Orient and Greece in sixth grade. In the first metamorphosis my mother was compared to one of the Gorgon sisters, crowned with a head of poisonous snakes. In the second, to Leda, whose gentle beauty seduced the most powerful of gods. As soon as I began to speak, the faces of my father, my sisters, my mother's friends, and even Sandrino dropped, expressing surprise, astonishment, and disbelief. But my mother's handsome mask remained impassive. Sitting upright in her chair, she adopted her favorite pose with her left hand against her neck clasping her chin. Her eyes were half closed as if she were concentrating on hearing me out.

Dressed in a sky-blue tunic I paraded and postured in front of her for a good forty-five minutes.

Suddenly she stared at me. Her eyes glistened with a shiny film that soon burst and tears trickled down her powdered cheeks.

"So that's how you see me?" she asked without a hint of anger.

Then she got up, crossed the living room, and went up to her room. I had never seen my mother cry. Not even when she broke her arm during a fall on the stairs. At first, it was a heady feeling that resembled pride. I, ten years old, the littlest, I had vanquished the Beast that threatened to swallow the sun. I had halted the stampede of oxen off the boats from Puerto Rico. Then, I was gripped with dismay. God, what had I done? I had not learned my lesson. My troubles with Yvelise had not been enough. You must never tell the truth to those you love. Never. Never. You must portray them in glowing colors. Give them reason to admire themselves. Have them believe they are what they are not. I ran out of the living room and raced up the stairs. But the door of my mother's bedroom was closed. However much I cried and hammered on the wood with two fists and even two feet, it remained shut.

I spent the night in tears.

The next morning my mother pretended that nothing had happened. She didn't brush my hair any more roughly than usual and stuck a pink bow on my four braids. She rubbed palma christi oil on my legs to make them shine. She had me revise my homework. When, crying my heart out, I put my arms around her neck, explaining I didn't mean to be spiteful and pleading forgiveness, she asked in an icy tone: "Forgiveness? Forgiveness for what? You said what you thought."

Her self-control was indicative of how hurt she'd been.

10

The Loveliest Woman
in the World

In the cathedral of Saint-Pierre and Saint-Paul our pew was number thirty-two in the center aisle. As a small child, I could have walked to this refuge blindfolded, past the beadle who frightened me every time he struck the ground with his mace and guided by the flood of organ music and the smell of lilies piled on the high altar. The pew was narrow. The wood was shiny as if polished with wax. The back was very high. So high I would have had to get up on my knees, if I had wanted to see what was going on behind, but that was forbidden.

My father, who had dealings with the Freemasons, did not accompany us to the cathedral. He stayed home in his shirtsleeves and had his friends over—all miscreants, my mother would sigh. Together they smoked cigars, and once in a while downed one or two shots of rum. From our house to the cathedral it was only a few minutes' walk in a straight line. You just had to cross the Place de la Victoire. But my mother stopped every ten paces to greet or converse with an acquaintance and we had to wait for her. In any case there was no question of me running off or jumping around, for she locked her hand in mine. Sandrino always dawdled at the back of the group, looking mournful, being the atheist he claimed to be. We marched up the front steps in unison and entered the cathedral two by two, my mother and I leading the procession. When we drew level with our pew we made the sign of the cross and I tried to mimic my mother's elaborate gesture. Then we kneeled on the razor-sharp edge of the prayer stool. We kept our heads between our hands for a few minutes, imitating my mother. Then we sat back. The cathedral was as bright as a glasshouse, and the silence was broken by muffled coughs and infant cries. Finally the organ sounded and the priest emerged surrounded by an assembly of choirboys in red robes, swinging incense holders left and right in great swoops. I think all my brothers had been choirboys, one after the other, except for Sandrino, who had refused outright. God and the church were the only topics of contention between my parents. But they never quarreled about it. My father thought it only natural for a woman of standing to be religious and my mother thought it inevitable that a man wasn't.

Although I was extremely coquettish and loved dressing up, I did not like going to church. I had to wear a hat that yanked my hair, put on patent leather shoes that pinched my toes, cotton, knee-length socks that made me hot and, worst of all, keep silent for over an hour, which was torture as I always bursting to tell a story. In my discomfort I often closed my eyes and managed to doze off after the reading from the Gospel. But this annoyed my mother and she shook my arm like the branch of a coolie plum tree. My mother who, according to my sisters, let me do anything, showed no lenience whatsoever regarding behavior during mass. She was determined I should remain awake until the liberating sentence of *Ita missa est.* So as not to fall asleep I would hum a song in my head. Sometimes, alas, I forgot myself and it would slip out of my mouth, whereupon I would receive a firm tap. For the nth time I examined every detail of the plaster statues standing in their niches: Saint Anthony of Padua with his tonsure. The Infant Jesus astride his prayer book. Saint Theresa of Lisieux with eyes raised heavenward under her crown of rosebuds. The Archangel Michael wearing sandals—how unwise!— to trample a serpent. I turned my gaze toward the stained-glass windows illuminated by the sun. Nothing new there either. Some yellow, red, and blue. I tried to pick out friends of my parents among the sea of faces. I recognized some of them, all solemn and dressed to the nines. Dr. Mélas, who had just treated me for an ear infection. Monsieur Vitalise who kept toads in his pharmacy bottles. As I grew up I couldn't help noticing how few black or colored faces there were in the center nave of the cathedral under the ceiling in the shape of an upturned boat. They clearly stood out as if they had fallen into the bowl of milk in the nursery rhyme we used to sing naively:

> A black woman who was drinking milk,
> Said, "Oh if only I could dip
> My face in a bowl of milk
> And become whiter
> Than all the French,
> Ai, ai, ai!"

White Creoles everywhere you looked. White Creoles in the pew in front, white Creoles in the pew behind. From all four corners of La Pointe. Men, women, and children. Old, young, and infants in arms. You never saw so many as at high mass. You'd think the cathedral belonged to them. That the Good Lord was a close relative.

I did not feel any hostility toward the white Creoles, despite the episode with Anne-Marie de Surville, which at that time I had conveniently pushed to the back of my memory. My parents did not mention them any more than they told me stories about zombies or blood-sucking *soukouyans*. Once school was over, it never crossed my mind to linger with my white classmates. If our paths crossed, our eyes never met. One Sunday, I don't know why, I began to take a closer look at the white Creoles around me.

I knew that in Creole they were called *zorey* or "red ears." And it was true that the men and the boys had large, red, jug ears. The women attempted to hide them under their heavy curls and the girls under their ringlets and ribbons. Nonetheless their pointy ears stuck out in comical or threatening fashion on either side of their hats. My eyes roamed up and down the rows of faces, all similarly stamped with a pasty yellow complexion, bumped up against the imperial protuberance of noses and scanned the razor-thin lips. It was then, thanks to my playful exploration, that my gaze fell upon a very young woman wearing a black, straw pillbox hat upon her tawny hair, her forehead half covered by a veil, with velvety cheeks and a rosebud mouth. She was wearing a beige linen two-piece suit with a cameo pinned to her lapel. I had never seen anything so perfect. For the remainder of the mass I couldn't keep my eyes off her. At one point her eyes met mine and, to my deep regret, quickly turned away with an expression of indifference. She hadn't noticed me. After the *Ita missa est* she rose from her pew, piously knelt down, crossed herself, and clasped the arm of a man. The following Sunday, seated in my observation box, I saw her arrive accompanied by her family, still on the arm of her equally young husband, who sported a mustache and a rather commonplace expression, quite unworthy in every respect of possessing such a treasure. This time she was dressed in white lace, her pillbox hat replaced by a wide-brimmed hat, and her cameo by a choker of respectable proportions. With what seemed to me to be an incomparable grace she took her seat in pew number twenty-nine, not far from ours. Like a detective I noted down the number. I was dying of curiosity. Back home I asked my mother who was this family of white Creoles in pew number twenty-three. I knew that my mother and her good friends were first-rate genealogists. They masterfully memorized the tree of weddings, alliances, and separations. A great deal of their conversation consisted of updating it, so much so that they could have been of considerable help to any notary laboring over the problems of inheritance and succession. My mother knew the answer of course.

"They are the Linsseuils. A good match, they have just married Amélie to the son of the owner of the Grosse Montagne factory."

She was about to switch to something else when, on second thought, she swirled round and asked in surprise why was I interested in those people?

"Because," I retorted passionately, "I think Amélie is the loveliest woman I've ever seen."

And I added without heeding her expression: "She's my ideal of beauty."

A deathly silence. She remained speechless. She called for my father, who was joking in the living room, and summoned my brothers and sisters, who were quietly staring out of their bedroom window. She expounded on my crime: How could my ideal of beauty be a white woman? Weren't there any people of color who deserved this distinction? Even a mulatto woman, a *capresse*, or a coolie would have been acceptable! My father, who knew it was unwise to contradict my mother, for once took my defense. Wasn't this much ado about nothing? I was still very young. My mother would not hear of these extenuating circumstances. I already had a mind of my own. I knew what I was doing. There then followed a few well-chosen words along the lines of what later would become Black Is Beautiful. My cheeks were on fire. I felt especially ashamed since my one loyal ally, Sandrino, seemed to approve. I retired to my room. In a way I guessed my mother was right. And yet I wasn't guilty. I hadn't admired Amélie because she was white, although her pink skin, her blue eyes and wavy hair were part and parcel of everything I admired about her. It was all beyond my understanding.

The next Sunday, out of the corner of my eye, I saw Amélie kneel down and cross herself at the entrance to her pew. I did not turn to look in her direction.

I understood that her beauty was out of bounds.

11

Forbidden Words

At the end of one particular year, my mother came down to sit at the dinner table evening after evening with watery eyes and swollen eyelids. Adélia devotedly filled her plate, but my mother did not touch a thing and quickly went back up to lock herself in her room, where we could hear her moan like a wounded animal. My father stayed put. But he wore an appropriate expression for the circumstances and sighed deeply between spoonfuls of thick soup. After dinner, Adélia took her up an herb tea, recognizable by its peppery scent, and stayed with my mother for hours on end.

In the meantime, I waited for her impatiently. Sandrino and I were not allowed to cross the street without her and take up our places in the yard of the Clavier family. In the early days of December we used to get together as neighbors and with heads raised toward the starry firmament, belt out the Christmas carols, sometimes until midnight. Even Granny Driscoll brought a bench and sat down in a corner. My parents, however, who never attended these gatherings, let us take part. Carol singing was the only concession they made to the local folk traditions. In their opinion, although the rhythm of the carols was as boisterous as the beguines and Creole mazurkas, joyously beat out on basins and saucepans, the words were very proper. In proper French. Real French. Even today I can still sing my favorite *"Michaud veillait la nuit dans sa chaumière,"* word perfect. As well as *"Voisin, d'où venait ce grand bruit?"* *"Venez, divin Messie, venez, source de vie,"* and *"Joseph, mon cher fidèle."*

For me, the reason for my mother's condition was a mystery. She was not sick, because my father had not called for Dr. Mélas. She had not argued or quarreled with anyone such as a neighbor, a colleague, a stranger, at the Dubouchage School, in the street, in a shop, or at the movie theater. What could have upset her? Sandrino finally whispered in my ear that the husband of my sister Emilia had left her. They were going to divorce.

Divorce?

I did not know my sister Emilia very well. For years she had lived in Paris, and the only time I met her was when we stayed in France. Over twenty years separated us; we did not have much in common. My father, who seldom showed his feelings, melted whenever he mentioned his firstborn, his very own favorite. He described her sense of humor. He boasted of her intelligence, her charm, her sweet nature, compliments that seemed like so many barbs directed against poor Thérèse, whom the family agreed was sulky and ugly. Brandishing photos from her album, my mother claimed that Emilia was her spitting image. She had married Joris Tertullien, the son of a well-known and wealthy dignitary from Marie-Galante. Their picture sat proudly on the piano. They had gotten married in Paris, two anonymous students, probably to avoid any family hullabaloo. I knew they had lost a child. They were of little interest to me. My parents were very flattered by this alliance with the Tertulliens and referred to it at the slightest opportunity. In their eyes, the union of Emilia and Joris was like the marriage of two dynasties whose family trees were of equal importance. Deep down, I imagined it symbolized my mother's revenge on an island her own mother had left in dire straits and poverty.

Shortly after the wedding of Emilia and Joris, on August 15, the day of the patron saint of Grand Bourg, Thérèse, Sandrino, and I were shipped off to the Tertulliens as a testament to our new family relations. It was my first visit to Marie-Galante, my very own Desirada. The stretch of sea was very rough. The *Delgrès*, which sailed daily from La Pointe, was packed. The ship surged up to the crest of the waves, then violently plunged several feet to the bottom of the swell. The passsengers vomited everywhere. The more experienced had brought along paper bags, which they stumbled to throw over the railings. They often missed their mark and the contents of the bags burst onto the deck. What with the crowd, the swell, and the stink I would have fainted if Thérèse had not stuffed slices of lime in my mouth. After three and a half hours of agony, the island finally emerged from the water. White cliffs dotted with shacks, which clung like goats at the most amazing angles, rose up out of the waves. The sea, as if by magic, became calm and the *Delgrès* gently moored alongside the jetty. Monsieur and Madame Tertullien were a surprise to us. Quite the opposite of our parents. Modest, smiling, and affable. The wife, shuffling along in her sandals, was wearing a straw hat tied under her chin. The husband, huge, but debonair, won my affection immediately when he swooped me up calling me "the pearl in the casket." Despite their rough-and-ready manners they lived in the finest house in Grand Bourg next to the church, and every morning a line of supplicants formed in front of their door to beg for favors from Monsieur Tertullien. This week spent on Marie-Galante was an enchantment. The Tertulliens, who had an only son, spoiled me more than was permissible. Every morning, Madame Tertullien asked me conscientiously what I would like to eat as if I were a princess in a fairy tale. Monsieur Tertullien bought me a doll that opened and shut its eyes. I had never imagined such freedom, and when I saw my mother again dressed to kill waiting for me on the wharf in La Pointe, I wept the hot tears of an escaped prisoner who had been sent back to jail. Too shrewd not to be fooled, she sadly commented on the ingratitude of children's hearts. From then on the Tertulliens often sent us baskets brimming with root vegetables, Congo peas, and lima beans, and bottles of white rum at fifty-five proof that flavored Adélia's cakes.

Divorce?

To my ears, the word had an obscene connotation. It meant that a man and a woman who had kissed on the mouth and snuggled up together under a mosquito net each went their own separate ways and behaved like two strangers. Despite Sandrino's express recommendation, I could not keep such information to myself and I told Yvelise. Yvelise gave her own version. If two people had had children, they were split up like chickens in a barnyard. The girls stayed with their mother. The boys left with their father. This Solomon's judgment made me indignant. I objected. And what if a boy preferred to remain with his mother and the girl leave with her father? And what if a brother or sister couldn't live without each other? Yvelise stuck to her opinion. She knew: Her mother often threatened to divorce her father.

A few days later my mother returned home from school, beside herself. We could hear her fuming in her room. She had good reason to do so. During recess some colleagues of hers, hearing of my sister's misfortune, had conveyed their deepest sympathy. My mother had taken it very badly and issued a sharp rebuff. What misfortune were they talking about? Her daughter's coming divorce? Wasn't it obvious that by leaving Emilia, Joris Tertullien had once again demonstrated the irresponsibility of the Caribbean male?

The very next day a stream of neighbors poured into our house. My mother had hardly returned home from school when they began knocking on the door. Finally she held court, sitting stiff as a poker on the corner sofa in the living room until dinner. The visitors were mostly mothers who feared a similar fate for their children or were already lamenting it. But there were also old maids, wives and women who had been spurned, battered, and cheated on, embittered and in revolt, ready to spit venom on the male species. My mother did not see in this assembly a mark of sympathy. Instead, according to her, these women had come to spy on her in her grief caused by her daughter's misfortune, to revel in it and rejoice. So evening after evening these visits plunged her into a rage mixed with bitterness.

When the stream of visitors began to dry up and my mother had other things on her mind than keeping up appearances, one question surfaced. Where had the leak come from? Who had revealed the information that my parents had firmly intended to keep secret for some time to come? My tears gave me away. I pitifully confessed that I had confided in my inseparable friend Yvelise. Everyone realized that Yvelise had told Lise, who had considered it too juicy to keep to herself and shared it with her colleagues at the Dubouchage School. From there, the news had spread throughout La Pointe. I must say, to be truthful, that neither my father nor my mother laid a hand on me. I was neither punished nor bullied. And yet I felt more ashamed and mortified than if my father had unbuckled his belt and given me one of those thrashings he reserved for Sandrino. My parents recited to me the age-old song. We were constantly under threat from all sides. Divorce. Distress. Sickness. Financial troubles. Failure. If in the unlikely event any of these occurred, it must be kept private because, as I had just witnessed, our enemies were always on the lookout for an opportunity to take advantage of our misfortune. The same old leitmotif. How could such a gifted little girl like myself not understand that? Why was my attitude so negative?

I never heard a single word of compassion for Emilia. I never knew what caused the distressing epilogue to her marriage to Joris. In fact, nobody cared. Emilia was guilty. Her failed marriage to the Tertullien heir tarnished my parents' reputation. It was a breach in the wall of pride that our family was intent on building around them. For this reason, there were no grounds for pitying her.

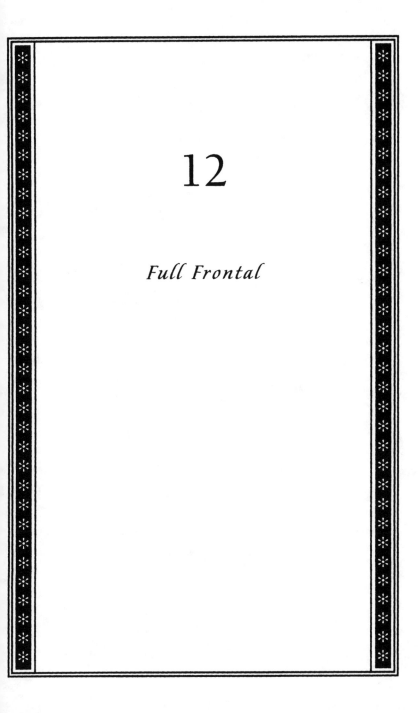

12

Full Frontal

The only relation my mother kept in regular touch with was one of her cousins from Marie-Galante. Twenty years her junior he went by the heavenly name of Séraphin. He was a hefty, taciturn, and awkward boy who reeked of his rustic origins. When he spoke, his French sounded like Creole and he got his genders and possessive adjectives wrong. My father made a point of giving him his old clothes, and so on Sundays he arrived for lunch in newly soled shoes and shirts with threadbare collars and cuffs that we recognized. He never failed to turn up with a bunch of pink roses for my mother's birthday; the woman he religiously considered to be his benefactor. This dutiful boy was the laughing stock of my brothers and sisters. During Sunday lunch whenever my mother offered him a second helping he would never fail to reply with a polite shake of the head: "Thank you, Cousin Jeanne, I've eaten my fill!"

I, on the other hand, quite liked him. I suppose I took pity on him. Since nobody troubled to converse with him, while waiting for lunch he took refuge in my room and emptied his pockets to give me presents: flutes carved from bamboo stems, ox carts from avocado stones, and once a long-stemmed pipe made out of lichee seeds he'd apparently varnished. I am sure it was Séraphin who initiated my passion for Marie-Galante. His father was a woodworker in Saint-Louis, and he would describe to me the shavings that curled around his fist amidst the smell of fresh wood. He also described the billy goats as they gamboled through the undergrowth, the sea caves whose cliff walls plunged from a breathtaking height into a watery inferno, and the purple realm of the ocean as far as the eye could see. I gave up asking him about my mother. He knew nothing about her. When, at the age of seventeen, he left his flat island his parents had been bold enough to petition this relative whom they had never met but had heard so much about. It was thanks to my mother that Séraphin had become a model employee, rising through the ranks of the postal service, as she liked to remind him.

Year after year we saw Séraphin grow up, and year after year he watched us do the same. We saw him take a wife. One Sunday he brought us Charlotte, his betrothed. She was not from Marie-Galante, but from the Grands-Fonds on Grande Terre. She was a good match for him, as pot-bellied and big-bottomed as he was, in her dark red, mutton-sleeved dress. It was obvious that Sandrino, sitting on the opposite side of the table, paralyzed her with his probing eyes and that my parents' manners terrified her. Scared of making the slightest grammatical mistake, she kept her mouth shut throughout the meal. She reluctantly uttered a few inaudible words when she was presented with a second helping of the beef with capers that Adélia was so proud of. After much debating, the family concluded that she had murmured: "I've had enough."

Since I was good for every occasion, my parents dragged me along to the wedding of Séraphin and Charlotte. The blessing was given at the church of Saint-Jules in the district known as l'Assainissement. I never went much farther than the Place de la Victoire and only crossed the Vatable Canal by car when we drove to our country house in Sarcelles. So this was the second time I found myself in a working-class neighborhood. At that time the Assainissement District was a strange mosaic of plain wooden shacks haphazardly perched on loose stones and a gigantic building site from where, it was hoped, modern apartment blocks, a grand hotel, the Banque de la Guadeloupe, and a clinic would emerge. The church of Saint-Jules, with its weathered wooden façade and its roof in the shape of a ship's hull, seemed to me a marvelous sight. Ringed by hovels, however, it was an unassuming and genuine place of worship. It was overflowing with fresh flowers, lilies and gardenias, and the daylight streamed in through its tall louvered windows, which arched to a point. The families of Séraphin and Charlotte, two clans each numbering fifty or so, were ridiculously dressed up. Yet I didn't have the heart to laugh at all that taffeta and lace. On the contrary! I felt a deep sympathy for the little girls my age, their hair tightly curled with burning hot irons and white Vaseline, proud as peacocks in their cheap shiny satin dresses and their high-heeled patent leather shoes. I wished I could have been one of them. I wished I could have climbed into one of the rented country buses which, as soon as the ceremony was over, would drive the wedding party to the Grands-Fonds. I could imagine the gargantuan feast of blood pudding, curried goat, squid, conch, the bottles of rum, the laughter and the band playing boisterous beguines, and all the fun I had experienced seemed pale in comparison.

Shortly after their wedding Séraphin and Charlotte disappeared. My mother told us that Séraphin had been transferred far from La

Pointe to the northern part of Grande-Terre. To Anse-Bertrand or Petit Canal. For a period of several years my mother was sent a good many pictures, which she dated and fixed in her album. Pictures of their children, all boys, born in quick succession. At first, they came naked lying on their stomachs. Then they came dressed in sailor's suits standing on sturdy legs. One July while we were spending the holidays in Sarcelles a letter informed my mother that Séraphin was now manager of the post office in Sainte-Marie. She took it to be good news. Sainte-Marie was only about fifteen kilometers from Sarcelles. At that time in Guadeloupe visits were unannounced. Relatives, close or distant, best friends, or acquaintances turned up without warning and expected to be welcomed with open arms. Miraculously, they always were. So one Sunday after mass my mother thought it quite natural to pay a surprise visit to Séraphin and Charlotte. We loaded baskets of vegetables and fruits, bourbon oranges, fig bananas, and soursops into the Citroën. Carmélien, our handyman, settled in behind the wheel, since my father suffered from cataracts that turned the pupils of his eyes blue, and had given up driving. It took us over an hour to cover the few kilometers that twisted and turned along the shore. My mother anxiously kept an eye on the needle of the speedometer. Sainte-Marie would have gone unnoticed on the map of the island if Christopher Columbus's caravel had not landed there in 1493. To mark the event, a statue of our Discoverer stands in the middle of a small square named Place du Souvenir. Séraphin and Charlotte lived behind the post office, an ill-kempt house with its veranda cluttered with bicycles and all kinds of broken appliances. However loudly Carmélien sounded the horn and my mother called out, nobody appeared on the veranda. After a while she decided to go in, with me hard on her heels, and as soon as we stepped inside we felt something was wrong. The living room was in an unimaginable state of filth and disorder—a real pigsty. A groaning, broken by violent moans and hoarse yells, came from one of the rooms. It was as though a hog had finally had its day and was hanging by its back legs losing its blood over a bucket. My mother anxiously cried out to no one in particular, "Anyone at home?"

Finally, Séraphin emerged from one of the rooms. Wearing a butcher's apron around his waist, bearded and disheveled, his face bloated, he had grown even fatter. Recognizing my mother he seemed stunned, then began to cry: "Cousin Jeanne! Cousin Jeanne!"

It so happened that at that very moment Charlotte was giving birth to their fourth child. As it was a Sunday Séraphin had been unable to track down the midwife. Charlotte was losing pints of blood, tiring herself out, no longer managing to push. Helped only by the servant woman, Séraphin was going to a lot of trouble and getting nowhere. I have already mentioned that my mother was not someone to lose her nerve. Without a moment's hesitation she laid down her handbag, removed her wide-brimmed hat, and dragged Séraphin into the bedroom. I stayed behind in the living room, wondering what to do with myself. There were in fact some books on the shelves of an old bookcase. But could I sit down and start reading under such circumstances? It was then that I heard giggles and muffled whispers. I opened another door. Standing on the bed, three children no higher or bigger than a tuft of Guinea grass were jostling each other in fits of laughter in front of a small opening cut into the wall. Seeing me they scattered in all directions. I came closer, and likewise stuck my face to the hole in the wall.

I who lived with blinkers on my eyes with a mother who never told me anything, not a word about periods or menstruation, I who had to rely on Yvelise's stories to discover that babies are not born in cabbages, dressed in pink or blue blouses, I saw with my own two eyes a full frontal, life-size childbirth. A nauseating smell struck my nostrils. As bloated as a blimp, Charlotte was lying spread-eagled on the bed. Her center, gaping open like a hosepipe, was spurting blood. From her mouth came a constant lament *"An moué! An moué!"* (Help! Help!) broken at regular intervals by screams that made your blood curdle. A servant woman, likewise dressed in a butcher's apron, was running around the bed sobbing and wringing her hands. My mother wrapped herself in a towel, pushed the others aside, and shouted with authority: *"Ou kaye pousé à pwézan!"* (Now push!)

It was the first time I had heard her speak Creole. Despite the pestilential smell, despite the sight of all this blood, a horrible fascination glued me to the wall. I fought over the observation post with the other three children, who had returned to the attack and were intent on seeing as much as they could. Charlotte was now screaming nonstop. I saw the head of the baby appear. I watched as it came out. I saw its entire body sticky with mucus and fecal matter. I heard its first yell while Séraphin beside himself exclaimed: *"An ti fi! Mèsi Bon Dié!"* (It's a girl! Thank the Lord!)

Incapable of bearing it any longer, I slowly collapsed to the floor in a faint. The children brought me round by dousing my face with a pitcher of water. Once a certain order had been reestablished, the baby in its cot and the mother in her silk nightgown, my mother and I found ourselves face to face. "What a visit! My poor darling, what have you been doing all this time?"

I pretended I had read a novel that was lying around. I'm sure she was no fool. I was still upset, my voice was feeble, and my legs were shaking. She quickly changed the subject and began to criticize the way Séraphin and Charlotte kept house. Had I ever seen such filth? Really, all those years she had set them an example had been wasted. When I told Sandrino about the incident he was utterly mortified he had not been present. For once his little sister had gotten the better of him. I had been enriched by an experience he would have trouble bettering.

The child born that day was baptized Maryse. I was chosen as godmother.

13

School Days

I must have been thirteen. Yet another stay in the *métropole*. The third or fourth since the end of the war. I was less and less convinced that Paris was the capital of the universe. I led a life as regular as clockwork, but in spite of that I missed La Pointe and the blue of the harbor and the sky. I missed Yvelise, my classmates, and our rambles under the sandbox trees on the Place de la Victoire until six in the evening, the only distraction we were allowed at home. Six was the hour when darkness fell and when, according to my parents, anything could happen. Looming up from the other side of the Vatable Canal, males hungry for sex might solicit us virgins from respectable families and taunt us with obscene words and gestures. In Paris I also missed the love letters that the boys managed to slip me, despite all the precautions taken to protect me.

Paris for me was a sunless city, a prison of dry stones and a maze of Métros and buses where people remarked on my person with a complete lack of consideration: "Isn't she adorable, the little Negro girl!"

It wasn't the words "Negro girl" that hurt. In those days it was a common expression. It was the tone. One of surprise. I was a surprise. The exception in a race whom the whites obstinately considered repulsive and barbaric.

That year my brothers and sisters entered university and I was left to play the only daughter, a role that I had difficulty accepting as it meant even more motherly interference. I was a student at the Lycée Fénelon, two steps from the Rue Dauphine, where my parents had rented an apartment. As usual, my insolence had turned all the teachers in this prestigious but grim establishment against me. Among my classmates, however, and for the same reason, I had won the status as ringleader and made quite a few friends. We hung out together as a group within a square bordered by the Boulevard Saint-Germain, the Boulevard Saint-Michel, the murky waters of the Seine, and the art galleries on the rue Bonaparte. We would dawdle in front of the Tabou Club, where the memories of Juliette Greco still lingered. We would browse the books in La Hune bookstore. We would peer at Richard Wright, as monumental as a bonze, sitting on the terrace of the Café de Tournon. We hadn't read any of his books. But Sandrino had told me about his political engagement and his novels, *Black Boy, Native Son,* and *Fishbelly.* The school year finally came to an end and the date for returning to Guadeloupe was fast approaching. My mother had bought everything that could be possibly bought. My father was methodically filling metal trunks painted green. At the Lycée Fénelon there was no tradition of taking it easy or letting off steam at the end of term. But now that the curriculum had been wrapped up there was a feeling of lightheartedness, even high spirits in the classrooms. One day the French teacher had an idea. "Maryse, give us a presentation of a book from your island."

Mademoiselle Lemarchand was the only teacher I got on with.

More than once she had given me to understand that her classes on the eighteenth-century philosophers were intended especially for me. She was a Communist whose front-page photo in *L'Humanité* we circulated among ourselves. We did not know exactly what the much bandied Communist ideology entailed. But we guessed it was a complete contradiction of the bourgeois values embodied, as we saw it, by the Lycée Fénelon. For us, Communism and its daily *L'Humanité* smacked of heresy. I believe Mademoiselle Lemarchand thought she could understand the reasons for my behavior and was giving me the chance to analyze them. By inviting me to talk about my island, she did not mean simply to amuse us. She was giving me the opportunity to liberate myself from what, according to her, was weighing on my heart. This well-intentioned proposition, however, plunged me into a deep quandary. It was, let us recall, the early fifties. Literature from the French Caribbean had not yet blossomed. Patrick Chamoiseau lay unformed in his mother's womb and I had never heard the name of Aimé Césaire. Which writer from my island could I speak about? I resorted to my usual source: Sandrino.

He had changed quite a lot, Sandrino. Unknown to anyone, the tumor that would carry him off was gnawing at him malignantly. All his mistresses had forsaken him. He lived in extreme solitude on the ninth floor of a building without an elevator in a wretched garret on the Rue de l'Ancienne Comédie, for my father had cut off his means of subsistence in the hopes of bringing him back to the benches of the law faculty. He scraped by with the money my mother sent him in secret, haggard, short of breath, and feeble, typing manuscripts with three fingers on a wheezy typewriter and invariably getting the usual rejection notices from publishers.

"They are not telling me the truth," he fumed. "It's my ideas they're scared of."

Naturally he was a Communist as well. A photo of Joseph Stalin complete with mustache was pinned to his wall. He had even gone to an International Communist Youth Festival in Moscow and had come back lost in admiration for the domes of the Kremlin, Red Square, and Lenin's tomb. As usual he did not let me read his novels, and I tried without much success to decipher the titles scribbled on the back of the dog-eared folders. For me, he made an effort to regain his luminous smile and the reassuring manners of a big brother. We delved into his books piled haphazardly on the furniture and the dusty floor. *Gouverneur de la Rosée* (Master of the Dew) by Jacques Roumain. About Haiti. I would have to describe voodoo and speak on a bunch of things I knew nothing about. *Bon Dieu rit* by Edris Saint-Amand, one of his last friends, who was Haitian as well. We were about to give up when Sandrino came across a treasure. *La Rue Cases-Nègres* (Black Shack Alley) by Joseph Zobel. Set in Martinique. But wasn't Martinique the sister island of Guadeloupe? I went home with *La Rue Cases-Nègres* under my arm and locked myself up with the little hero José Hassan.

Those of you who have not read *La Rue Cases-Nègres* have perhaps seen Euzhan Palcy's film *Sugar Cane Alley*, based on the book. It's the story of one of those little ragamuffins my parents dreaded so much, who grows up on a sugar-cane plantation amid the pangs of hunger and deprivation. While his mother hires herself out to some white Creoles in town he is brought up with many a sacrifice by his grandmother, Mama Tine, a cane bundler in a dress quilted with patches. His only escape route is education. Fortunately he is intelligent. He works hard at school and is about to move up the social ladder at the very moment his grandmother dies. I cried my heart out reading the last pages of the book, the finest I believe Zobel ever wrote.

> It was her hands which appeared to me on the whiteness of the sheet. Her black hands, swollen, hardened and cracked at every joint, and every crack coated with an indelible mud. Encrusted fingers, cramped and bent, their ends worn and hardened with nails thicker, more callused and shapeless than hooves. . . .

For me, the entire story was quite exotic and surrealistic. In one go I was saddled with slavery, the slave trade, colonial oppression, the exploitation of man by man, and color prejudice, which nobody, except occasionally Sandrino, ever mentioned to me. I knew of course that whites did not mix with blacks. But I attributed that, like my parents, to their immense stupidity and blindness. Elodie, for example, my maternal grandmother, was connected to the white Creoles sitting two pews down from us at church who never cast a look in our direction. Tough luck for them! They were depriving themselves of the joy of being related to someone like my mother, the success story of her generation. I could in no way apprehend the tragic universe of the plantation. The only times when I vaguely rubbed shoulders with the rural world were during the school holidays spent at Sarcelles. My parents owned a country house, what we called a "change-of-air" house, in this once peaceful corner of Basse-Terre, quite a handsome estate that got its name from the river that ran through it. Here for a few weeks everyone, except my mother, who was always on her guard, her hair carefully straightened under her net, wearing a golden choker, played at being *bitakos* or country bumpkins. As there was no running water, we scrubbed ourselves with clumps of leaves, standing naked next to the water tank. We relieved ourselves in a *toma* or thunder box. In the evening we lit oil lamps. My father, who loved the country, would slip on a shirt and a pair of twill khaki pants, stick his head under a *bakoua* hat, and arm himself with a cutlass, which he hardly used except to cut through the Guinea grass. We children were overjoyed at running barefoot and being allowed to dirty and tear our old clothes. We raced through the savanna looking for black hogplums and pink guavas. The cane fields seemed to welcome us with open arms. Sometimes, intimidated by our city-dweller looks and our French-French way of talking, a country yokel would respectfully hand us a Kongo cane that we tore into with our teeth.

Yet I was scared to make such a confession to my classroom. I was scared to reveal how José and I were worlds apart. In the eyes of this Communist teacher, in the eyes of the entire class, the real Caribbean was the one I was guilty of not knowing. At first I rebelled, believing that identity is something you have to accept whether you like it or not, whether it suits you or it doesn't. Then I gave in to outside pressure and slipped into the old clothes I was being handed.

A few weeks later, I gave a dazzling presentation in front of the whole class, leaving them spellbound. For days, my pot belly had rumbled with hunger. My legs were bowed. My nose was filled with snot. My mop of kinky hair had reddened from the effects of the sun. I had been transformed into Josélita, the sister or cousin of my hero. It was the first time I had cannibalized a life. Something I would soon take a liking to.

Today, I am convinced that what I later called somewhat pretentiously "my political commitment" was born at that very moment, the moment I had been forced to identify with poor José. Reading Joseph Zobel, more than any theoretical discourse, opened my eyes. I understood then that the milieu I belonged to had absolutely nothing to offer and I began to loathe it. I had become bleached and whitewashed, and because of it, a poor imitation of the little French children I hung out with.

I was a "black skin, white mask" and Frantz Fanon was going to write his book with me in mind.

14

A Forest Sojourn

That year, my mother's arthritis forced my parents to skip Sarcelles and spend their "change-of-air" in Gourbeyre because the waters at Dolé-les-Bains were said to be very effective. I greeted the idea with enthusiasm, for in the end Sarcelles had become too familiar. I knew all its nooks and crannies, the leech-filled meanderings of its river, its backwaters where guavas and hogplums grew and the taste of every type of mango: hairy mango, grafted mango, Julie mango, bellyfull mango, and rose mango. When I was little, apart from San-drino, my playmates had been the three motherless children of the watchman. We had now grown up and I had lost the art of playing.

Gourbeyre is situated to the south of Basse-Terre. I remember it took a whole day to get there, although it was only sixty or seventy kilometers from La Pointe. My mother woke me on her return from dawn mass and we set off before sunrise, the car loaded with baskets, cases, and trunks. A real migration! Once past the Rivière Salée, the journey at first held no surprises—traveling along a flat, pleasant road, green hills silhouetted against the horizon, bridges spanning sleepy rivers, goats gamboling with ears cocked, and zebus lowing as the cars went by. Suddenly, just before Capesterre, not yet named Belle Eau, the strange sight of an Indian temple striped with the colors of Mariamman, drew me out of my daydreaming. So that, too, was Guadeloupe?

Then the landscape began to change. Hills rounded their bellies. Banana groves with long shiny leaves replaced the fields of sugar cane and rose in terraces up the hillsides. Gushing streams from the waterfalls flooded the side of the road. The air turned cooler. At a bend in the road, we happened upon the panorama of Les Saintes, the islands of Terre-de-Haut and Terre-de-Bas, floating in a circle on the blue of the sea. I gazed wide-eyed and felt that, without realizing it, I had been born in an earthly paradise. The house my parents had rented in Gourbeyre was of modest appearance. What grieved my mother was not that it needed a fresh coat of paint, that its veranda was too narrow, that water did not flow in the shower, that the W.C. was a revolting little hole at the back of the yard, or that the kitchen faucets leaked. But the fact that it was next to a shop, barely bigger than the palm of your hand, which was well stocked with an assortment of items from wheaten cookies, cassava flour starch, and codfish, to kerosene, turpentine, and, above all, bottles of white rum, much to the delight of the neighboring rum guzzlers. This hit home the following morning when we awoke to hear an already inebriated customer exchange words with the cashier. In fact, my parents had fallen victim to misleading advertising, a common experience for so many holiday makers throughout the world. The "stunning view" in the ad looked out onto a wall and the "five minutes from the beach" turned out to be a forty-five-minute walk. The misunderstanding was especially cruel because finding themselves cramped into four rooms of a near hovel adjacent to a rum shop, they felt outside their class.

Their appearance had been downgraded to the dreaded rank of second-rate Negroes. According to the rigid social geography at that time the region of Trois Rivières, Gourbeyre and Basse-Terre belonged to the mulattos. Saint-Claude and Matouba were the realm of the white Creoles who vied for it with the Indians. My parents' place, however, was on Grande-Terre. It was here that the blacks had evolved and made their mark in politics as well as in every other domain. Too young to know whether there was a deliberate attempt to encourage us to go back where we came from, I do know we were totally ignored. However much my parents drove around in their Citroën C4, however often my mother wrapped her neck ostentatiously in her golden choker and my father swaggered around with his Legion of Honor ribbon that had such an effect in La Pointe, nobody paid us any attention. Holding parasols aloft, everyone shook hands, embraced, and chatted in front of the church as mass ended. We, however, crept through the crowd without receiving or giving the time of day. At dusk, my parents strolled past elegant dwellings with iron gates that never swung open for them, then returned home to sit on the shabby veranda of their rented villa as long as the mosquitoes permitted. They retired to bed at nine after drinking an infusion of lemongrass tea. Against the advice of my father who weathered the situation stoically, my mother took out her frustration on Madame Durimel, the owner. A dragon of a woman who right in the middle of lunch would regularly send her son to deliver us a letter as inflammatory as the one she had received. This exchange of correspondence lasted throughout our stay. After two weeks, Madame Durimel agreed to make a few repairs. But the water stubbornly refused to bubble out of the showerhead and we washed in the yard with buckets and basins as best we could. Things took a turn for the

worse when Marinella, who acted as a servant and came with the
furniture, placed a burning hot iron on my father's shirtfront. My
mother decided to dock her wages, whereupon Marinella handed in
her apron and with Madame Durimel in tow arrived in the middle
of a meal to pelt her with abuse. It was incredible. In La Pointe,
everyone cowered in front of my mother.

I, on the other hand, loved Gourbeyre. At last, I was an anonymous
person. Nobody knew me, nobody paid any attention to me. I could
have run barefoot in the street if I had wanted to. Three times a
week, while my father stayed home reading *The Count of Monte Cristo*
yet again, my mother walked up to take the waters at Dolé-les-Bains
and took me with her. What could have been a chore turned out to
be a delight. In a castlelike setting out of *Sleeping Beauty* nestled the
recently closed Grand Hotel. It was a huge wooden building painted
green and ringed by two balconies. Once, I managed to slip inside
and discovered two-way mirrors, threadbare carpets, and heavy lo-
custwood furniture eaten by termites. Following my mother from a
distance, I rambled under the shade of the trees sapped by epiphytes,
amidst the warm smell of humus, to a pool poetically called the Bath
of Love. While she cautiously lowered herself in to soak her legs, I
returned to daydream under the canopy of silk and cotton trees. I
stubbed my toes against their roots sticking up like buttresses or
crutches. I lay down to doze on the carpet of moss and lichen and
woke with a start when, worried out of her mind, my mother would
be desperately calling my name. Somehow I became friends with
Jean and Jeannette, neighborhood twins whose one-story house was
a wretched shack. They were the children of a bus driver who drove
his country bus on the route Gourbeyre–Basse Terre–Saint-Claude,
swearing like a trooper. My parents frowned on this friendship. But

since I was so isolated they could not do much about it. They did forbid me, however, from going on an excursion up the volcano and another to a string of lakes, much to my fury. I was increasingly exasperated by the way they controlled my life. As a peace offering they allowed me to accompany the twins to a literary afternoon organized by the parish.

The program was not very exciting. Recital of poems by Emmanuel-Flavia Léopold and a certain Valentine Corbin, who had sung the praises of Dolé-les-Bains, plus one or two scenes from Molière's *Imaginary Invalid*. But I was in seventh heaven between Jean and Jeannette, my mouth stuffed with crumbly cake. The room was full. Fathers, mothers, brothers, sisters, aunts, and uncles dressed to the nines squeezed in to applaud the talents of their young family members. While waiting for the show to begin, the audience roared with laughter, chatted and joked. Finally, the curtain opened. I listened to the sentimental lines we have all learned by heart at elementary school:

> *Je suis né dans une île amoureuse du vent*
> *Où l'air à des odeurs de sucre et de cannelle . . .*
> (I was born on an island in love with the wind
> Where the air is scented with sugar and cinnamon.)

The place was abuzz with noise and light-heartedness. I think I understood there and then what my parents were lacking. These mulatto women were no lovelier than my mother, even though they were more light-skinned and their thick, ample hair cleverly styled. Their smile revealed teeth which were no more pearly. Their skin no more velvety. They were not better dressed. Their jewelry no heavier or richly worked. These men, these mulattos, were no more conceited than my father. Yet they possessed something that would always be missing in my parents. My parents were never natural. It was as if they were constantly trying to control and master something lurking deep down inside them. Something that at any moment could escape and cause the most terrible damage. But what? I remembered Sandrino's words, which I still hadn't quite grasped: "Papa and Maman are a pair of alienated individuals."

I finally felt I had got to the heart of the matter.

The stay in Gourbeyre lasted six weeks, six weeks of taking the waters. Back home in La Pointe, my mother buried this experience deep in her memory and any reminder came out as a series of sighs, gesticulations, and shaking of the head. For me, however, it was a mine of ever magical stories that I never tired of telling to Yvelise.

15

Free at Last?

For my sixteenth birthday my parents gave me a bicycle, a Moto-bécane, a pretty blue bike with silver mudguards that put wings on me.

The stay at Dolé-les-Bains made me want to unlock the cage I had been in ever since I was born. I realized that I did not know my own island. I realized that all I knew of La Pointe was a narrow rectangle. As I was becoming increasingly rebellious, my parents understood they had to allow me room to breathe. At the age of seventy-eight, my father had practically lost his eyesight. Although invisible threads guided him as long as he remained inside the house, once he was outside, his vision blurred. He could neither cross the street nor find his way home. Since my mother had lost patience with him, he would go off to Sarcelles, the only place where he felt at peace, and like a wild man of the woods, would go for days without washing or a change of clothes. As for my mother, she had taken a turn for the worse. After a bad bout of flu, she had lost most of her hair and stuck poorly-made *postiches* as black as ink on her head, and these clashed with the rest of her thinning salt-and-pepper hair. Her religious devotion reached new levels, which Sandrino's death less than a year later only accentuated. She missed neither dawn mass, high mass, low mass, sung mass, nor vespers, rosary, Tenebrae, stations of the cross, or the month of the Virgin Mary. She made novenas, penance, fasts, rolled the beads of her rosary, took confession as well as communion. When she was not deep in devotion she quarreled with me. For absolutely no reason. For absolutely nothing. I can't remember why we constantly squabbled. I can only remember I always had the last word. I lashed out at her with my sharp tongue and she invariably ended up in tears sobbing: "You're a viper!"

Alas, the feeling of empowerment I had when I was ten had vanished. These tears had become a daily, commonplace sight that no longer drew compassion. My early years had been bathed in sunlight from my brothers and sisters, secretly in revolt against my parents. My adolescence was tinged with the colors of old age. I found myself alone with two antiquated individuals whose moods I did not understand. There reigned a morbid atmosphere in the house. The third floor had been sealed off, doors and windows nailed shut since nobody lived there anymore. I wandered miserably through a series of empty rooms, once Thérèse's and Sandrino's. I leafed through books gathering dust on the shelves. I opened cupboards where old clothes still hung. I sat on beds with sagging mattresses. It was as if I were roaming a graveyard in remembrance of those I had lost. Sandrino had just been admitted to the Salpêtrière hospital. My mother had convinced herself his illness was benign, but she guessed the outcome. She did not have the strength to make the journey to France, and the thought of him there was killing her. Thérèse, on the other hand, was taking her revenge. Her letters were short and few-and-far-between. She had married a medical student from Africa, who was the son of a reputed doctor in his own country. Yet my parents, so prestige conscious, disapproved. Even as a child, Thérèse's doings had never met with their approval. And then Africa was too far away on the other side of the earth. My mother spoke of ingratitude and selfishness. She had not even bothered to put the photos of little Aminata on the piano, even though she was her first granddaughter.

At fifteen, I looked at myself in the mirror and found myself ugly. Ugly as sin. Stuck on the top of a lanky body was a melancholic, taciturn face. Hooded eyes. Untidy, skimpy hair. Lucky front teeth but not a sign of any good luck. The only saving grace was a skin of velvet that acne had dared not attack. Boys no longer turned their heads in my direction, which pained me because I had started to appreciate handsome specimens of the male species. Gilbert Driscoll had been transformed into a dandy with brilliantined hair parading around his young girlfriends in the neighborhood. Friends were as scarce as admirers, since Yvelise had left school to go to work for her father. We no longer saw each other and my mother badmouthed her behind her back, claiming she had men and would soon be saddled with a belly. At the *lycée,* where I was more uppity than ever, teachers and students alike were scared of me. Isolated, I sharpened my barbs like arrows that I hurled at everyone. As I was about to sit for my second baccalaureate a year in advance, I appeared the incarnation of intelligence combined with spitefulness.

Once I possessed my Motobécane I did not need anyone. I no longer bothered my head about my reputation. I pedaled and pedaled, soon venturing outside La Pointe. I discovered the low, swampy shoreline of Vieux Bourg at Morne-à-l'Eau, half covered with muddy seawater, and its mangrove inhabited by wader birds all dressed in white. I pedaled in the other direction toward Bas-du-Fort and the spectacular sight of the tall, chiseled limestone cliffs and the golden sands I had never had the chance to see before. As for beaches, I only knew Viard with its black volcanic sand like the dirty nails of an unwashed foot. Three or four times during the long school holidays we would spend the day there, my mother decked out in an ensemble handmade by her seamstress Jeanne Repentir, my father wearing long underpants and immodestly baring the white hair on his chest. A servant woman hired for the season from Petit-Bourg would heat up the *colombo* curry on a fire amid four stones and we would picnic under the wild almond trees. Sometimes, one of the locals would prowl around and peer at this family tableau with curiosity. I lay for hours on the sand wide-eyed, grimacing under the scorching sun. I longed to plunge into this great expanse of blue. Sandrino had taught me how to swim, a bit like a dog, but I didn't have a swimsuit. This item of apparel appeared only much later in my wardrobe, and I had grown too big for the Petit Bateau panties I used to wear. After the Bas-du-Fort, I ventured farther, as far afield as Le Gosier. I had already read Virginia Woolf's *To the Lighthouse*. I was no longer inventing stories and made up for it by avidly reading everything I could lay my hands on. So I stared at the little island anchored a few cables' length from the shore and transformed it into a literary object, intertexture of dream and desire. Once I struggled as far as Sainte-Anne, in those days a peaceful little village undisturbed by tourism. I slumped down on the beach. Sitting crosslegged beside me, impervious to my strange expression, the fishermen joked while mending their nets. The market women were selling skewers of tench and blue marlin to their customers. Children as black as tar were swimming naked. I dozed off, mouth open, and awoke to find dusk was falling. All around me the beach was deserted and the tide was up.

As a rule I tried to be home before nightfall. This was the first time I had let darkness creep up on me. I was scared. Scared of the winding road. Scared of the shape of the houses suddenly transformed into she-devils, scared of the menacing trees and the banks of raggedy clouds. So I sped home in a frenzy, my knees touching my chin, leaning flat out on the handlebars. And without understanding why, the speed went to my head. I felt free, full of the freedom I was soon to enjoy. Within a year I would leave Guadeloupe, separated from my parents whom I had never left for more than two weeks. The prospect both exalted and terrified me. What was I going to study? I felt no calling. My teachers had destined me for the preparatory classes of France's elite schools; in other words I would be back at the Lycée Fénelon. This meant leaving one prison for another. And yet beyond the jail they intended me for I could catch a glimpse of open doors I would squeeze through. When I arrived out of breath at the Rue Alexandre-Isaac, my mother was waiting for me in the living room. She began her imprecations. What was I doing racing around like crazy under the sun? Wasn't I ugly enough and black enough as I was? I looked like a Kongo girl. If it was a man I was looking for, I was wasting my time.

I swept past her without a glance and locked myself in my room. She went on prattling. After a while, she ran out of breath and words and struggled up to the second floor for she was increasingly racked with the arthritis she has left me with. I could hear her bump into the furniture and climb into her bed, which creaked like a boat being put to sea. Under the deceptive colors of pity, all the love I had for her surged into my heart and almost suffocated me. I went into her room without knocking, which was forbidden. Lying in the middle of her bed she was propped up against a pile of pillows, for she complained of breathlessness during the night. Her prayer book lay open in front of her. She had removed her *postiche* and there were bare patches on her scalp. She was old and alone. My father had left for Sarcelles at the beginning of the week. Alone and old. I climbed onto the bed like I used to do when I was small, when nothing was refused me, when nothing was out of bounds. I hugged and hugged her and showered her with kisses. Suddenly, as if a signal had been given, we both began to cry. For the beloved Sandrino who was dying so far away. For the end of my childhood. For a certain life we knew was over. For happiness of sorts.

I slipped my hand between her now withered and useless breasts which had breast-fed eight children, and we spent the whole night together, her clinging to me and I curled up against her side amidst the smell of old age and arnica, lost in her warmth.

That is how I want to remember her.

16

The Mistress and Marguerite

One September 4 in the mid-1950s I found myself back in Paris, already muffled up in its fall colors. Not particularly overjoyed. But not unhappy to be there. Kind of indifferent. Like meeting up with an old acquaintance.

I left my former self ashore as soon as I set foot on the deck of the *Alexandria,* a banana boat that made the crossing in ten days. We were a dozen passengers, boys and girls, going to study in France. I was the youngest at sixteen and everyone treated me like a child prodigy. The atmosphere was morbid. No flirting, dancing, or joking, and we were desperately homesick. Moreover, there was no entertainment on board. We killed the morning hours by reading, slumped in the deckchairs facing the ocean. After lunch everybody shut themselves up in their cabins for siestas that lasted until dinner. Then, crowding into the smoking room, we halfheartedly played *belote.* I never imagined how much I was going to miss my mother. I realized she was "my North, my South, my East and West, my working week and my Sunday rest" as W. H. Auden says in his poem, *Funeral Blues.* Separated from her, I lost my appetite. I emerged from sleepless nights expecting to find myself curled up against her breast. Every day I wrote her pages and pages begging her to forgive me for my bad behavior over the years and repeating to her how much I loved her. On arrival in Dieppe, I posted ten letters at once. It was some time before she answered. Then, after that, she sent me short, terse notes which invariably ended with the trite words: "Your maman who is thinking of you."

Even today I am still trying to find consolation. Her surprising indifference was probably pathological. It must have been the first signs of that mysterious illness which one morning confined her to her bed and carried her off a few days later in her sleep.

In Paris I lived on the Rue Lhomond, just steps away from the Rue Mouffetard in the heart of the old city. Thérèse, who had become my guardian, had found me a room in a respectable hostel for young girls from the Antillean upper class, mainly from Martinique. Surrounded by dark or blond, curly- or wavy-haired mulatto girls, and high-yellow girls with green, gray, or blue eyes, I was the only one with black skin and kinky hair. The other two girls from Guadeloupe were Danièle, who could pass for white at a quick glance, and Jocelyne, tossing over her shoulders the flowing tresses of a Hindu princess. It didn't bother me in the slightest. Since I thought I was the ugliest girl on earth, I made no comparisons. Yet I was struck by one incongruity. Although my color assimilated me with the ragamuffins, the cane cutters, the cane bundlers, the fishermen, the market women, the dockworkers, and goodness knows who else, I felt more removed from them than from the light-skinned damsels I was friends with. At least they chattered away in Creole, burst into peals of laughter, and shook their butts to the rhythm of the beguine. It was as if their parents had never drummed into them how to behave. It was as if they did not share my parents' contempt for local traditions. How could this be possible? Sandrino was dead, I had nobody now to guide me. Lost in the labyrinth of my thoughts I sported a morose and taciturn expression. I gave nobody the time of day. As soon as dinner was over I locked myself up in my room papered with reproductions of Picasso and listened to Beethoven's "Ode to Joy" and the Brandenburg Concertos. Fairly quickly, however, I made friends with Jocelyne, who stood out from the others. Born and educated in Dakar, where her father was a magistrate, she barely knew her parents' home island of Guadeloupe. Caribbean customs and habits amused her and she had no scruples about making fun of them. She had nicknamed our fellow islanders at the hostel "the darling doodoos" and swore they considered the Sorbonne a hunting ground for husbands. She believed she was intellectually superior to everyone except me, which was flattering. Together we idolized Gérard Philippe and on weekends we never missed a performance at the Théâtre National Populaire. We shared the same passion for the movies. I envied her her beauty, her self-assurance, and the way she clamped her cigarette-holder between her teeth when we sat at the café terraces where I would never have dared set foot without her, and from where she intimidated the boys with her brazen eyes plastered with mascara.

As in La Pointe, there was no room in my life for the unexpected. I never took the bus. I stumped through the Latin Quarter from the Rue Lhomond to the Lycée Fénelon. Once classes were over, I sat down on a bench in the Luxembourg Gardens holding a cornet of hot chestnuts, and the memory of my mother brought tears to my eyes. When night fell, I set back off for the hostel in time for dinner served amidst the din of a refectory filled with bursts of laughter and the sound of voices. Like a zombie I lapped up my soup.

At the *lycée* I discovered the rigors of a program for preparing the entrance examination to France's elite schools. Since I never opened a book or never went near the Sainte-Geneviève library, I was practically last in everything. In class, yawning over thankless Greek or Latin translations, or forced to meditate over Proust's insomnia, I could hear life's heartbeat throbbing and throbbing far from this hothouse of boredom. The world was out there, all around me. It was vibrating. But how could I find my way there? The teachers all agreed to leave me to my laziness. Their attitude said it all: This little Guadeloupean had no place here and was no candidate for France's top schools. Only Madame Epée, the French teacher, took a different approach. She was a somewhat buxom, platinum blonde, squeezed into a fur coat, who as soon as she set eyes on me took an instant dislike to me. My apathy and indifference exasperated her. She was thinking about the best way to torture me when, at the end of October, a new student arrived. Her name was Marguerite Diop, and she was the daughter of a high official from Senegal. As short as I was tall. With a round face and spiteful eyes. So skinny that the pullovers she slipped on to keep out the cold, one over the other regardless of elegance, did nothing to fatten her up. All smiles. Always ready to entertain the schoolyard with an African tale. To share a candy, a gift from one of her numerous aunts. She was an excellent student, hard-working and lively. In a word, my opposite. Madame Epée took advantage of our difference and used it against me. Henceforth, French class became a zoo where the keeper showed off her caged animals. An arena where the animal tamer forced them to do tricks. Villon, du Bellay, Chateaubriand, and Lamartine, the whole of French literature became a pretext for the kill. Occasionally, the Benin bronzes were called in to the rescue or Monomotapa's frescoes. Madame Epée assigned me a role. Always the same one. It was obvious I embodied the degradation of Africa transported to the New World. Once they had crossed the ocean, the values that Marguerite incarnated so wonderfully, languished. Gaiety and humor vanished. Intelligence and feelings were snuffed out. Grace and elegance flew away. All that remained was dull-wittedness, aggressiveness, and sullenness. Madame Epée had no qualms about interrogating us one after the other, assigning us the same composition and, with the class as witness, commenting on our performance. Without knowing it perhaps, she had joined the long line of missionaries and colonial administrators who have ridiculed and reviled the "detribalized African," the "trousered nigger," while refusing to acknowledge that Marguerite, educated at a Catholic boarding school in Dakar and admitted to one of the best *lycées* in Paris, was no "purer" than I was. I must say that apart from three or four girls, oblivious to what was being perpetrated in front of them, the other students did not appreciate these circus games. They demonstrated their dislike for Madame Epée through their lack of discipline, their insolence, and their writing on the blackboard. They were actively sympathetic toward me. I was flooded with invitations to lunch and weekends at their parents' country homes. I accepted. Yet, back at the hostel, I couldn't help thinking I had been forced into playing the role of the token talented black girl. No, I did not come out of a cane field. Yes, my parents were local dignitaries. Yes, I had always spoken French at home. My classmates would have liked me to rebel and respond to the attacks of my aggressor. They did not understand that, deprived of my mother and my big brother, I no longer had the strength.

Constantly paired as opposites, Marguerite and I should have been bitter rivals. We weren't. Madame Epée brought our contrasting characters closer together. Sitting in the Luxembourg Gardens, shivering under our pullovers, Marguerite dismissed my arguments with a sweep of the hand: I was not the only one Madame Epée had a personal grudge against. She was a racist who hated both of us. Divide and rule, it was a common colonial policy. Her speeches on the virtues of Africa were pure hypocrisy. As insulting as her wild theories about the degradation of the Caribbean. Marguerite suddenly interrupted her scholarly explanation to point out to me her "cousin," Cheikh Hamidou Kane, a brilliant young economist, hurrying up the Boulevard Saint-Michel, and her "cousin" Cheikh Anta Diop, finishing a formidable book on the truth about the Egyptians, and my solitude melted at the idea that every black was related.

She often invited me to the home of one of her aunts, the wife of a Senegalese parliamentary member. A twelve-room apartment on the Avenue Marceau, cluttered with children, visitors, genuine relatives, hangers-on, and swan-necked women perched on high-heel shoes. At any time of day or night fish with rice was served on priceless dishes, chipped by the careless hands of servants. Camille, one of her "cousins," fell head over heels in love with me. He was short and stocky, supremely intelligent, a future executive at the World Bank. "In twenty-five years," he predicted, "our countries will be independent." He was mistaken, it took only five. It felt good to be wanted at last, kissed on the mouth and fondled. However, I wasn't ready for Africa. At the end of the second term Marguerite disappeared. A rumor went round that soon turned out to be true. She had gone back to Senegal. To get married. We even learned she had been pregnant and had strapped herself tight all winter. As a consequence, Madame Epée forgot about me to rail against her former pet. Class after class she transformed her into a lamentable symbol of women of her race, spineless and devoid of intellectual ambition. In a few years she would find herself overweight, chewing on a toothpick, and dragging her sandaled feet to nowhere.

Sitting on the dunce's bench, I had resumed my daydreaming. I imagined Marguerite with the features of a Senegalese woman from an old engraving I liked. She was lying on a sofa, reclining against multicolored cushions, in a garden filled with haughty, barbaric-looking flowers. Her head was wrapped in an enormous blue kerchief. On her feet she wore bootees with ankle ties. She was opening her taffeta corsage and offering her breast swollen with milk to her baby. Her sprawling opulence flouted Madame Epée's diatribes. At the same time I was hoping for a letter, a card, some sort of sign to confirm my depiction of her happiness.

She never wrote to me.

17

*Olnel, or Welcome
to The Real World*

At the end of the school year I was sent down from the preparatory class for admission to France's top school, the Ecole Normale. It was just what I had expected. My mother made no comment. My father sent me a letter, a model of its kind, informing me I had tarnished his name. I believe it was about this time I was getting a reputation in the family, which I eventually accepted as true to character, that despite my intelligence I would never get anywhere.

In November I enrolled at the Sorbonne like a prisoner touching ground after her escape. I slipped radiant and anonymous into its overcrowded lecture theaters. With one kick I sent the classics flying. No more Latin, Greek, Old French, and Middle French. I opted for English literature. It was less fusty. And then I had discovered those great poets, Keats, Byron, and Shelley. Their poetry went to my head.

> *Was it a vision or a waking dream?*
> *Fled is that music.—Do I wake or sleep?*
> > *Keats,* "Ode to a Nightingale"

141

I became fascinated by the cruel stories of their lives, realizing that suffering is the only real price to pay for artistic creativity. Thanks to my newfound freedom I met up with old friends from La Pointe, from the time of my first communion. My classmates from school, now in their second year of preparatory class, had not forsaken me. Françoise, who liked to think she was as Red as her father, a professor at the Sorbonne, had learnt from him how to hold forth on anticolonialism. For my birthday she gave me a copy of *Notebook of a Return to My Native Land*. Césaire's poetry did not have the same revolutionary effect on me as Zobel's lucid prose a few years earlier. At first reading, I decreed it was in no way comparable with my English idols. Yet Françoise's enthusiasm as she declaimed passages on the terrace of the Mahieu Café was contagious. Gradually I opened the floodgates and let myself be carried along by the torrent of images. I accompanied Françoise to the meetings of the Sociétés Savantes on the Rue Danton, where French and African Communists were debating a new law for independence drafted by Gaston Defferre. I was bored by these dry speeches. I did not even notice one of the speakers, a union leader from Guinea by the name of Sékou Touré.

Less than two months later I was back to square one. My enthusiasm had flared up and died like grass on a bonfire. English literature was not just Shakespeare and my trio of rebel geniuses. *The Forsyte Saga* and the novels of Jane Austen depressed me even more than Tacitus and Plato. And then there was Old English and Middle English. I bade the Sorbonne good riddance. I don't recall exactly how I spent my time: I do remember a lot of it was spent in the Mahieu Café and the bookstores. But although my life was enjoyable it was by no means carefree. Far from it. I lived in a desert of affection. Too many years separated me from my sisters, Emilia and Thérèse. Their feelings of affection for me were merely lukewarm. In their eyes I was the youngest child overly spoiled by our aging parents, but life, thank God, would take care of that. The Saturday ritual was lunch at Emilia's. In order to avoid conversation while I ate she shut herself up at the piano in her bedroom. She was a marvelous player who could bring tears to my eyes. I knew she had dreamed of becoming a concert pianist. Instead, my father had steered her into studying pharmacy, which she never completed. Before the good-bye kiss, she would never fail to slip me a few banknotes, enough for the average family to live on. Every time I got the impression it was her way of asking forgiveness for not taking more interest. I spent one weekend out of four at Thérèse's pretty, ramshackle place in the shadow of the basilica of Saint-Denis. When we were not quarreling, we had absolutely nothing to say to each other: She was too taken up with her little girl and her husband, and then I had always irritated her. She found me self-centered and indecisive. She thought I was supercilious, whereas deep down I was scared to death. I didn't have a boyfriend. The boy who was about to have an affair with me had been adroitly snatched up by Jocelyne under my very nose. This setback by no means helped develop my self-confidence.

I very quickly realized that I was better off in the company of solitude. Together we visited the exhibitions of Léonor Fini and Bernard Buffet. We stood in line for the Louis Malle films. Not at all intimidated, she came with me to those huge Parisian brasseries and waited while I swallowed oysters by the dozen, to the stupefaction of the other customers. She was with me when I leafed through the travel agents' brochures and decided to buy rail tickets. Together we roamed through England, Spain, Portugal, Italy, and Germany. In her company I broke a leg on a ski slope in Austria and was flown down to the valley by helicopter. We celebrated my seventeenth birthday in the general hospital. Admitted for what I thought to be a common case of appendicitis I was operated on for an ovarian tumor. The doctors in their dismay told me I almost didn't make it and that my chances of being a mother were exceedingly slim. I, who would later give birth to four children, cried my heart out at my future sterility. Even my body was giving up. Yet this hospital stay had its high points. In the bed next to mine was Madame Lucette, a street vendor who sold her produce on Rue Rambuteau. I listened to her with the fascination of a child who has just learned to read and is turning the pages of her first storybook. So that's how the other half lived! Madame Lucette proudly introduced me to her stream of visitors, and when they went into raptures over my French it didn't upset me. I prattled on even louder to please them. I showed them photos of my family, and everybody admired my mother's beauty. But once I had left the hospital my friendship for Madame Lucette did not survive lunch in the shack she lived in at the back of an alley in the Fourth Arrondissement. The pot-au-feu was excellent, but I was still the daughter of my parents.

In the spring, Jérôme, a friend from Guadeloupe who, unlike me, was diligently studying for his history degree, asked me to help him with the Cercle Luis Carlos Prestes. Who was Luis Carlos Prestes? A martyr? A politician? A cultural patriot? Today I still haven't got a clue. We frantically organized literary afternoons, conferences, lectures, and I began to take a liking to these activities that took up so much of my life. I even gave a lecture myself. On Guadeloupean culture. I forget what the reaction was. It was simply proof that at the time I was not afraid of talking on subjects I knew nothing about. The Cercle Luis Carlos Prestes flourished. I was asked to speak and write articles. I won a prize for a short story published in the Caribbean Catholic students' journal. In other words, although my university work was nil, I earned intellectual prestige among the students. That year I failed my exams miserably, and my father, furious, refused to pay for my return home to Guadeloupe for the long holidays. This decision, which had a certain logical justice to it, had terrible consequences.

I was never to see my mother alive again.

One afternoon at the Cercle was devoted to a debate on Haiti, where a certain Dr. François Duvalier was a favorite candidate for president. All I knew about Haiti was the Katherine Dunham ballet which I had admired a few years earlier sitting between Papa and Maman at the Empire Theater. I had no idea what everyone had against him, this François, except for his somewhat simian mask. Compared to his opponents, mostly *petit bourgeois* mulattos, I felt rather sympathetic to the color of his skin. My education had been *Noiriste* without knowing it.

In its entire existence, the Cercle Luis Carlos Prestes had never witnessed such a stormy session as that afternoon. The Duvalierists and the anti-Duvalierists, the black students and the mulatto students, almost came to blows. Jérôme and I were powerless to calm the frenzy, which was a complete mystery to us. Witnessing such passion made me feel envious. Oh, how I would have liked to be born in a real country, an independent country—and not this speck of an overseas territory! To fight for one's government! Have a presidential palace with all the glitter of a president! From one day to the next I struck up a friendship with two Haitian students in political science, Jacques and Adrien, who, whether you could believe them or not, fell head over heels in love with me. Well-read, they knew everything about their country: its history, its religion, its economy, its political and racial tensions, its literature and naive painting. Hard-working, these two bookworms made me ashamed of my inertia. I had a soft spot for Jacques, with his dimpled, protruding chin and his misty eyes. "You see," he would sigh, "life is like a Haitian telephone. You call Jacmel and you get Le Cap. You never get what you want." In his opinion, I would do better to study language and literature. It was he who gently guided me back to the Richelieu lecture theater where Professor Marie-Jeanne Durry was putting on her act. But Jacques and Adrien were, above all, the ghosts of Sandrino, two big brothers who had come back into my life. I couldn't make up my mind which one to choose. Both were spoiled sons from privileged families, well-mannered and reassuring in their identical duffle coats. Whereas the already impetuous and mixed-up side of me was longing for the unusual, the unknown, the dangers of a real life, I could imagine the life I would be leading in Pétionville or Kenscoff: a meandering river of boring tranquillity. I had no idea of the misfortune that lay in store for the Haitians: Jacques would be forced into exile in Canada while Adrien and his entire family would be among the first victims of the *tontons macoutes*.

One evening I followed my inseparables to the home of one of their fellow countrymen on the Rue Monsieur-le-Prince. There was a discussion about the peasant community, and we listened religiously to Olnel, a mulatto agronomist, who was describing the distress of the Haitian peasants in the Artibonite valley. At one point he broke off to congratulate me for an article I had written on Jacques Stephen Alexis's book *Compère Général Soleil*. If the Good Lord himself in Heaven had lifted the clouds to speak to me I could not have been more enraptured. That a man so handsome, so impressive, had noticed someone as mediocre as myself far exceeded my expectations. When we decided to leave for dinner, in my ecstasy I stumbled on the stairs, and beating Jacques and Adrien to it, he held my hand in a possessive grip.

It was here that my guardian angel, whom for years my mother had forced me to invoke, let me down. After so many prayers, rosaries, and novenas, he should have warned me, however small the sign, warned me of what Olnel had in store for me. But he remained silent.

We set off down the Boulevard Saint-Michel streaked with lights. Eyes wide open, the herds of cars roared down toward the Seine. That evening, very discreetly, my solitude broke away from me and bade me farewell. She had been my faithful companion for over two years. I no longer needed her. I had just met the real world, with its long procession of tribulations, failures, unspeakable suffering, and belated happiness. She remained standing at the corner of the Rue Cujas feebly waving her hand. I, however, in my ingratitude did not even look at her as I walked in a daze of illusions toward my future.

Printed in the United States
by Baker & Taylor Publisher Services